Excellent Buddhism

An Exemplary Life

Excellent Buddhism
An Exemplary Life

Kalu Rinpoche

Translation from Tibetan into French
François Jacquemart

English Translation
Christiane Buchet

ClearPoint Press
San Francisco, California

Excellent Buddhism
An Exemplary Life

Published by:
ClearPoint Press
PO Box 170658
San Francisco, CA 94117
USA

The original text of this book was published in French
and was entitled Bouddhisme Vivant
Copyright reserved for all countries:
Association Claire Lumière
12 Avenue Henry Barbusse
13760 St Cannat, France

Copyright ©1995 English Edition
ClearPoint Press
Printed in the United States of America
Printed on acid-free paper

Library of Congress Catalog Card Number: 95-78755
ISBN 0-9630371-4-5

Publisher's acknowledgement

The publisher gratefully acknowledges the generous help of Dwayne, Mei Yen, Gordon, and Robin Ladle; Parson and Yvoone Wong; Nelson and Teresa Kwan; Wilson and Wendy Tsai; Tau Fen and Shiao Yu Wu; Ge Shin and Celia Wang; Mike and Marie Chuang; Zimmer and Yun Ching Jan; Allen Jan; Tracy Jan; Ghih Ning Cheng Ru; Li Ping and Yu Ping Zhao; Jeng Long and Ying Mei Jiang; Tsai Farn Jan and Family; Chain Shu and Family; Thomas Jan; and Christiane Benedict.

Many generous friends helped in the different phases of the production. Thanks to Elson Snow, Jason Espada, Rosemary Gilpin, Juanita Hall, and Karen Graham. Special thanks are due to Chen-Jer Jan who did the layout of the book.

Introduction

This volume is part of a series of three books devoted to Tibetan Buddhism as seen through the teachings of one of the most revered masters of modern times, Kalu Rinpoche. The complete three-volume work is composed of:

Excellent Buddhism
Profound Buddhism
Secret Buddhism

The first volume, *Excellent Buddhism,* contains a number of biographical documents on Kalu Rinpoche, notably the remarkable memories of Lama Gyaltsen. The first volume also contains teachings dealing more specifically with daily life and with the relationship between Buddhism and the West.

The second volume, *Profound Buddhism,* presents the teachings on Hinayana and Mahayana as esoteric aspects of Buddhism. Profound Buddhism expounds on the absolute nature of mind, emptiness, and compassion; dealing with conflicting emotions; the situation of the individual in the cycle of existence; and karma. Finally, the third volume, *Secret Buddhism,* reveals the principles of Vajrayana, mantras, empowerments, the six yogas of Naropa, and so on. It includes important chapters on the *bardo* (the period of time between death and rebirth), Tibetan medicine, and initiation lineages.

Kalu Rinpoche, Lama of Light, came to France for the first time in 1971. Tibet, an inaccessible stronghold of highest spirituality, had remained separate up to this time, on the grounds that the rest of the world could not understand her. Kalu Rinpoche, then almost 70 years old, was the first, despite the skepticism of the majority of his peers, to believe that Tibetan Buddhism could have an impact in the West.

History proved that he was right. He taught many people during numerous trips until his death in 1989. A great number of them were captivated by his charismatic radiance and set out on the path of liberation. Kalu Rinpoche is no longer with us, but the wealth, depth, and diversity of his recorded teachings remain.

Unfortunately, these recordings are not accessible to the public. Not only is the lamp kept in the dark, but this treasury runs the risk of becoming lost. Reflecting on this situation, Lama Gyaltsen, Kalu Rinpoche's nephew, who was for 40 years Rinpoche's servant and then his secretary, asked Claire Lumière Publishing to collect and edit all the available teachings of Kalu Rinpoche. We have collected all the material that we have been able to find and, wishing to present the most accurate text possible, we have retranslated these teachings directly from the Tibetan. Lama Gyaltsen then asked ClearPoint Press to translate them in English.

We thank all persons who, in one way or another, brought their precious contribution to this publication. We more particularly want to thank the people of the following Dharma centers, who authorized us to use the teachings that have been given in the framework of their institutions:

Sogyal Rinpoche
Rigpa
22 rue Burq
75018 Paris, France

Tsenjur Rinpoche
Kagyu Kunkhyab Chuling
4939 Sidley Street
Burnaby, B.C., Canada V5J 1T6

Lama Gyurme
Kagyu Dzong
40 route circulaire du Lac Daumesnil
75012 Paris, France

Lama Gyurme
Vajradhara Ling
Chateau d'Osmont
Aubry-le-Panthou
61120 Vimoutiers, France

Lama Sonam
Kagyu Ling
Chateau de Plaige
71320 Toulon-sur-Arroux, France

Lama Tonzang
Karma Migyur Ling
Montchardon
38160 Izeron, France

Mrs Camille Vitrac
Kagyu Djong Sonam Ling
261 promenade des Anglais
06200 Nice, France

Karma Shedrup Gyamtso Ling
33 rue Capouillet
1060 Brussels, Belgium

Table of Content

Lama Gyaltsen's Memories

Lama Gyaltsen's life is remarkable. His father was a younger brother of Kalu Rinpoche. When Lama Gyaltsen was 10 years old, he met his uncle for the first time and soon became his close companion. At first, Lama Gyaltsen was Kalu Rinpoche's servant, then his secretary, and his disciple for more than forty years. Lama Gyaltsen was 53 years old when the death of Kalu Rinpoche, in 1989, seemed to definitively interrupt this long common road. However, a year later, a son was born to Lama Gyaltsen, and the child was recognized as the reincarnation of Kalu Rinpoche! A privileged witness of the life of his master in Tibet, India, and the West, Lama Gyaltsen was a confidant of other lamas and Kalu Rinpoche's mother. This is an account of the direct and indirect memories that he has wanted to share during a trip in France in the summer of 1992.

THE STORY OF A NAME

Kalu Rinpoche was born in Kham, the eastern province of Tibet, in a mountain chain called Tracho. His family's name was Ratak, a deformation of Ratsa, a term meaning "goat skin." To understand the origin of this name, we must go back to the time of the first Karmapa, Tusum Khyenpa.

Tusum Khyenpa was born to a poor family that bred animals on a mountain-side. In this region, one could distinguish poor people from the rich by their clothes. The poor families wore jackets of goat skin, while the rich families were clad in sheepskin. This detail is not without significance in our story.

When Tusum Khyenpa was born, no one realized that a holy man was being born. He was not granted any particular attention. Tusum Khyenpa kept herds, taking care of cows and goats like many children of his age. However, some events should have caused people to realize that he was not an ordinary being.

For example, water was rare in this region, which created difficulties for people and animals who needed it. One day, people noticed the young future Karmapa scratching at the ground around a boulder. He did this the next day and day after day after that. What was he looking for scratching like that? Children and other people began to wonder. However, water soon started to spring forth, to the astonishment of his friends who never thought that this dry place could conceal such water.

The future Karmapa was teased by other children because his family was poor. Sometimes, they chased him and threw stones. Again, he demonstrated his extraordinary nature on several occasions. One day, while he was seeking to avoid the rocks being thrown at him, he leaned for an instant against a cliff. Tusum Khyenpa's back left an impression on the cliff that is still visible to this day. Another time, while he was throwing stones back at his tormenters, the attackers ran away; but the stones hit them, regardless of how far they ran. These unusual events were regarded as the strange acts of a poor child who deserved no special attention.

However, since the young future Karmapa struck water in a place where its lack was sorely felt, he was shown some kindness by the people of the region, who found relief for themselves and their animals. Later, people began to notice that this water was endowed with healing properties. It especially healed those who had tumors of the digestive system. The spring still flows today, and people continue to come and drink its curative water.

When he became an adult, the future Karmapa went to central Tibet and was soon recognized as a lama of extraordinary capabilities. He had numerous disciples and his person gave rise to a great faith among the people. Because of the greatness of his realization, he was named "The One Who Knows The Three Times" (the past, the present, and the future).

The news of the Karmapa's achievements reached his native country where people finally decided that it was necessary to somehow show him their veneration. "This lama, whose reputation is now so great in Tibet, was a child of our village. When he tended the herds with us, we understood nothing of his magnificence. Now he is far away and we cannot meet him. We must find a way to evoke his presence among us. We need to find an object that could be the support of our devotion." They began to look for an object that had belonged to the child. Because of his poverty, however, Tusum Kyenpa had possessed very little. The villagers finally found the Karmapa's goat skin jacket that he wore when he was little. Wishing to make it into a sacred support, they decided to cut it into small pieces—one hundred thousand pieces,[1] according to the story. Then, they made the same number of small statues of the Karmapa and inserted the pieces of goatskin in them. They built a stupa in which to place the statues, and called it the Stupa of The One Hundred Thousand Statues with Goat Skin (Tibetan, Ratsa Kumbum Choten). The place became known as Ratsa, and the family linked with the first Karmapa inherited the name. Its members became the Ratsa; later the word was deformed into Ratak, which is the family name of Kalu Rinpoche.

Later, when the father and mother of the Karmapa passed away, the people of the region wanted to thank them posthumously for engendering such a holy being. They erected two small stupas on the right and the left of the main stupa in their honor. These three stupas are still visible today.[2]

---

[1] In the Tibetan tradition, one hundred thousand means the exact number or a very large number.

[2] In order to visit them, once in Kham, go to the city of Khanze, then to Ratakten where the three stupas are located.

FATHER & MOTHER: A MEETING SET BY FATE

Kalu Rinpoche's father was called Lekshe Drayang and had the title of Ratak Tulku, that is, the tulku of Ratak. He was the thirteenth incarnation of a lineage of tulkus stemming from the family of Ratak and, therefore, related to the first Karmapa.

Kalu Rinpoche's father was also the last representative of this lineage. Just before his death, Lekshe Drayang told his disciples that it would be useless to search for his tulku. Possibly, he would continue to work for the benefit of all beings, but this activity would be in other places and no longer within the family of Ratak. His disciples and benefactors insisted he manifest among them. Lekshe Drayang told them that they should not feel abandoned because he was leaving them a son far superior to himself. Nevertheless, in the region of Minyak near the Chinese border, a child was born who declared himself to be Ratak Tulku and who demonstrated the qualities of a great being.

In the retreat center of Tsadra Rinchendra (founded by Jamgon Lodro Thaye),[3] dependent upon Palpung Monastery, and directed by Situ Rinpoche, the young Ratak Tulku accomplished a three-year retreat, and then stayed there for a few more years.

In the course of his meditations, he had the experience of a *yidam* who told him. "You have to marry a woman, because your union will produce a child who will perform wonderful acts. The woman you will marry will be a *dakini* of wisdom whose name is the same as Drolma Karmo[4] (White Tara)."

---

[3]Jamgon Lodro Taye (1813-1899) was one of the greatest masters of Tibetan Buddhism of the nineteenth century. Famous for his realization as well as his immense scholarship, he worked for a better understanding between the different Buddhist schools of Tibet.

[4]In short, Drolkar.

During this same retreat, Situ Rinpoche offered him a statue of White Tara to show Ratak Tulku how much he appreciated his practice of years in retreat and to advise him to take White Tara as his main *yidam*. Situ Rinpoche thought that this practice would allow Ratak Tulku to gain experience and realization.

The same day Situ Rinpoche gave him this statue, a young woman arrived at Tsadra Rinchendra and offered Ratak Tulku a jar of the best curdled milk that one could find in the area. "What is your name?" asked Ratak Tulku to the young woman. "Drolkar,"[5] she answered.

The future father of Kalu Rinpoche found these coincidences odd. After the *yidam* talked to him, Situ Rinpoche gave him a statue of White Tara. The very same day a young woman with the name of the deity came to offer him curdled milk, in the same manner that the shepherdess Sujata had offered the milk to the Buddha Shakyamuni. He wondered if the young woman was not the one predestined for him. He asked her numerous questions about herself and her family. By her replies and his observation of her physical characteristics,[6] he was soon convinced that he was dealing with a *dakini*.

Nevertheless, some doubts remained. Would this union be beneficial? Would it really bear an exceptional son? Therefore, he asked the advice of the greatest lamas of the region, such as Situ Rinpoche and Dzokchen Rinpoche. They confirmed that these coincidences and signs were not random, but significant. He married the young woman, returned with her to his native village and moved into the residence of the Ratak Tulkus.

---

[5]Therefore, White Tara.

[6]*Dakinis* incarnated on earth are characterized by certain physical signs.

Drolkar, Ratak Tulku's spouse, was a member of a family related to Jamgon Lodro Thaye; her parents were Jamgon Lodro Thaye's benefactors. Situ Rinpoche would say later that not only did she have the same name as the deity White Tara, but that she was also Tara's emanation.

Very soon, Drolkar became pregnant. Lekshe Drayang immediately thought that the child to come would be the son announced by the *yidam*. It was a girl, and he was disappointed. A second pregnancy followed soon after. Lekshe Drayang was sure this time. He had no doubt that the *yidam's* prophecy would be realized, but again the child was a girl.

Thinking that he must not deserve to accomplish what had been announced by the deity, Lekshe Drayang sank into a deep sadness. Among the lamas he considered his root lamas, the main one was Khyentse Rinpoche from the monastery of Palpung. Lekshe Drayang decided to offer Kyentse Rinpoche everything he possessed—his house, his animals, his belongings, and his money—keeping nothing for himself.

His disciples and benefactors were both admiring and anxious. They pointed out to him that it was excellent to offer all his belongings to the lama, but added that they were concerned for him and his family as they would need at least a roof to shelter them! How did he envision that?

"I can do no good for anyone," replied Ratak Tulku. "It is useless for me to stay here. It is better if I leave. I have decided to take my wife and my two girls with me, go near the Indian border, and earn my living there by begging."

He left. However, two or three days later he was reached by emissaries of his disciples and benefactors who would not let their master live such a life. The discussion was intense. Lekshe Drayang flatly refused to return. His disciples begged him not to continue any longer, but at least to stay where they had found him. They would build a house for his use and provide whatever was necessary for his living. After arguing a long time, Lekshe Drayang accepted the compromise, but only for a one- or two-year period. After that, he would go elsewhere, probably where Jamgon Lodro Thaye had lived, because he had such great devotion for this teacher. The benefactors built a small house where Lekshe Drayang lived for a year or two. This house can still be seen today.

THE BIRTH

The retreat center of Tsadra Rinchendra was created by Jamgon Lodro Thaye, but his main residence was a small monastery called Dzongsho Gompa. It was there that Ratak Tulku went after honoring his commitment to his benefactors. He lived there with his family for some years following the death of Jamgon Lodro Thaye.

During this residence, Ratak Tulku had a dream one night in which Jamgon Lodro Thaye appeared and told him, "I will come to your place and borrow your house." This is the same night that the future Kalu Rinpoche was conceived.

Some months later, Ratak Tulku and his family moved to a small monastery called Ridrak Gompa, which was located in an area known for its variety and quantity of medicinal herbs. Ratak Tulku was a lama and a physician. In Tibet, physicians assumed the complete making of their pharmacopoeia.

One morning Ratak Tulku went to pick plants with his wife and his helpers. He noticed that on the right side of the house a great number of plants were blooming, although it was not the season for them to blossom. He saw that as an auspicious sign. Later that day, his wife did not feel well and he advised her to return home. It was not time to give birth, but it was better to be cautious. Ratak Tulku continued to collect plants.

Drolkar returned to the house. While climbing the stairs leading to the door, although not in pain, she felt that she was ready to give birth. She hurried inside and told her mother that the child was ready to be born. "Do not worry," answered her mother, "Where did you hear that children were born so easily?" Nevertheless, Drolkar went to her bedroom and the child was born without pain or delay.

"The child is born!" she shouted to her mother.

"What are you telling me?" replied the mother. "It is impossible!" Going to the bedroom, she added, incredulously: "So, where is it, this baby?"

She was forced to face the evidence. The child was there. Witnesses have said that birds started to sing in an unusual manner and a special rain, which Tibetans call metaphorically the "rain of flowers," fell on the house. Ratak Tulku, hearing the birds and seeing the rain, wondered what had happened. Returning home, he could not believe what his servants were telling him. His son was born.

It is also said that at the moment of birth, many wonderful signs manifested at the monastery of Jamgon Lodro Thaye and great lamas such as Situ Rinpoche, Dzokchen Kongtrul, and others felt particular inner experiences.

A FATHER DOES NOT GIVE UP HIS SON

When the child was older, his father taught him to read and write. The student appeared extremely talented and seemed to assimilate everything effortlessly. People in the neighborhood started to think that he was an extraordinary boy, without doubt a tulku. They told Ratak Tulku, who was known to be difficult. He told them that he did not want them to talk about his son in this manner. "My son, an extraordinary child? Perhaps. If so, he himself will reveal it. Meanwhile, I forbid you to speak of him as you do."

The child then took the monk robes[7] at the monastery of Begen. This monastery had no tulku, which was considered a disadvantage. The head of the monastery spoke with Ratak Tulku. "This child is your son and you are yourself a tulku; he seems to possess extraordinary qualities. Could we give him the title of tulku and enthrone him in our monastery?" Ratak Tulku gave a sharp answer, one more time: "You consider that the fact that this child is my son gives him a certain magnitude, and, due to his gifts, you would want to give him the title of tulku. I do not want to hear such words. If my son is a wonderful being, he himself will reveal it when he becomes an adult. It is useless to say that now. So, stop your comments and your projects. My son is now a monk; I do not want him to be treated differently than any ordinary monk at this time."

At other times, the young boy met such eminent lamas as Palpung Situ Rinpoche,[8] Dzokchen Kongtrul Rinpoche, Sechen Kongtrul, and Kado Situ. They also noticed his qualities, declaring that he certainly was a tulku. They asserted that he was no doubt an emanation of Jamgon Lodro Thaye.[9] It would be a good idea, they thought, to take him to Tsadra Rinchendra, the monastery founded by Jamgon Lodro Taye. Ratak Tulku did not change his answer. "Perhaps my son is a tulku. The future will tell. Meanwhile, I beg you not to

---

[7]Not exactly taking the monk vows, but observing the fundamental monk rules.

[8]Palpung Situ Rinpoche was the highest authority of the Kagyupa school in Kham. The other three lamas were eminent masters of the Nyingmapa school.

[9]Great lamas can create several emanations differentiated in body, speech, mind, qualities, or activity emanations. Kalu Rinpoche was identified as a tulku of the activity of Jamgon Lodro Taye, while other lamas were emanations of his body, speech, mind, or qualities.

proceed with an enthronement, and allow him to have the life of an ordinary monk."

Dzokchen Kongtrul and Setchen Kongtrul insisted. Admitting that it was not necessary to take the child to the monastery of Jamgon Lodro Thaye for enthronement, they wanted him to remain in their own monastery as a monk, particularly to provide him with careful training. Ratak Tulku remained firm. He would give his son to no one.

The young Kalu Rinpoche continued his studies at the monastery of Begen, and was so brilliant that at the age of eleven, he received the title of khenpo.[10] This was a new source of wonder and admiration for everyone. The intelligence of the child was so prodigious that, in little time, he assimilated that which normally requires the intellectual maturity of an adult and a dozen years of study.

Not only did the child devote this period to study, but he received the foundations (initiations, ritual readings, and explanations) of the traditional transmission from the great masters of all schools of Tibetan Buddhism. He also received major ordination from Situ Rinpoche, who gave him the name of Karma Rangjung Kunkhyab. This name prophesied that his activity would spread in a spontaneous (*rangjung*) and universal (*kunkhyab*) manner—in other words, over the entire earth.

THE MASTER WAITS FOR THE DISCIPLE

When he was 16 years old, Kalu Rinpoche prepared to accomplish the traditional three-year retreat, that is, the usual training for the lamas of the Kagyupa school. The druppen (retreat master) of the retreat at Tsadra Rinchendra was Lama Norbu Tondrup. Lama Norbu Tondrup lived on a small hill

---

[10]Title equivalent to "Doctor of Buddhism." Normally this requires a dozen years of advanced studies.

before arriving at the retreat center. In order to get there, it was necessary to pass through a door opening onto a small path leading to the lama's residence. This door protected his tranquillity. No one could get through without receiving the approval of the two guardian monks, the lama's nephews. They questioned all newcomers about their visit.

However, one morning, Lama Norbu Tondrup requested that his nephews leave the door open because he was expecting the visit of an exceptional guest. "You must let him come to me as soon as he arrives," he ordered.

Lama Norbu Tondrup did not divulge any more details to his nephews, but he explained the reasons to Situ Rinpoche. The previous night, the protector deity Chadrupa (Six-Arm Mahakala) had appeared to him. Chadrupa announced that a disciple would arrive the next day. This disciple, possessing all the required qualifications, would later benefit many beings. Chadrupa concluded by announcing that he was going to welcome the disciple holding a great *kata*[11] in his hands. This is why Lama Norbu Tondrup had given the order to keep the door wide open.

The two nephews awaited the arrival of this exceptional guest. They thought this could only be a person of high rank, such as the King of Dergue or perhaps a minister. The day was almost over, yet no one had come. At four or five o'clock in the afternoon, they finally saw an ordinary monk followed by two companions carrying loads on their backs. The nephews went to see Lama Norbu Tondrup. "It is late, and the guest you are waiting for has not yet come. However, a monk and two companions are coming, should we let them enter?"

"Yes, yes, let them enter," answered the lama. After having introduced the visitors, the two nephews went down

---

[11] A *kata* is a long scarf of white silk. Its length is a way to wish a long life; its whiteness witnesses the purity of the motivation of the person who offers it.

to the retreat center and told the monks that Lama Norbu Tondrup was expecting a special guest and that only an ordinary monk with two companions carrying his luggage had come. That made them all laugh.

The special visitor had indeed arrived. It was Kalu Rinpoche.[12]

RETREATS

During the three-year retreat, Kalu Rinpoche became Lama Norbu Tondrup's disciple. He received the complete transmission of initiations, ritual readings, and explanations of the Shangpa Kagyu lineage from him. During this same retreat, he also received many other initiations from passing lamas. After completing the retreat under the guidance of Lama Norbu Tondrup, Kalu Rinpoche returned home and, for two years, continued to receive teachings and initiations from a great number of lamas. He then decided to live as a complete recluse in places of retreat without telling anyone where he was.

Kalu Rinpoche's father was a famous physician. Up to the time of the retreat—with the exception of the last three years in Tsadra Rinchendra—Kalu Rinpoche had always helped his father harvesting plants, preparing remedies, and practicing medicine. From that time on, Kalu Rinpoche completely gave up all medical practices.

Kalu Rinpoche's places of retreat were, for the most part, so wild that an ordinary person would not have been able to stay there for a single day.[13] Take the case, for example, of the cave of Radung Pu, a cave an opening so large that wind

---

[12]One of the nephews was called Lama Tsewang. He was fond of retelling this episode when Lama Gyaltsen was little.

[13]In his childhood, Lama Gyaltsen visited some of these places of retreat. He only heard of the others.

continually howled through it. It was also populated by all kinds of insects that the darkness prevented one from seeing. How could one dwell in such a hostile place? Nevertheless, Kalu Rinpoche resided there for several years. Living in difficult places was not always a systematic objective. Sometimes, he stayed under a tent in a pleasant place near the family house where herds were grazing. During those years of retreat, he never worried about food, and apparently sometimes went a long time without eating.

THE DEER-GUIDE

Once, Kalu Rinpoche went on a retreat without taking any food. He did not tell his parents or anyone else where he was staying. Only two or three people had seen which direction that he had taken. His mother was extremely anxious. She would have preferred him to be in retreat at their place or, at least, at the monastery. Instead, he would go to uninhabited places without telling anyone where he was going and without food! Was he not going to die? Waiting for him became too difficult. His poor mother could not rest easy. Carrying food, she went to look for her son. She had gotten an idea of the place where Kalu Rinpoche was meditating by questioning people. She walked a long time in the mountains, until she could no longer see a path or know where she was going. She felt lost. What could she do? Should she continue to climb this unknown slope, or descend into the valley? What chance did she have of finding her son? She started to cry.

High above her, at the bottom of a boulder she could not reach, appeared a small animal, a kind she had never seen before. It was like a deer but not much bigger than a dog. Not understanding how such an animal could suddenly appear, she was surprised. At first, she thought nothing of it. She decided it would be better to return home because there was no chance of finding her son. Then, the animal quickly went away. Finding this strange, she changed her mind and decided to follow. Unable to see the animal, she followed the tracks it left in the snow. They led her high into the mountains until she saw smoke. At that instant, the animal and its track completely disappeared. When she saw the smoke, this sign of life, the mother felt an immense joy believing it revealed the presence of her son.

She called his name several times with all her energy, until finally Kalu Rinpoche appeared at the entrance of a cave. She hurried to him. Her happiness at finding her son was mixed with sorrow. She saw that he had nothing to eat, not even tea to drink. Besides drinking the red juice of the large leaves of a local plant, it appeared that Kalu Rinpoche took no food at all.

The mother was so worried that, hugging her son, she started to cry again. She begged him not to stay in this hostile place and said that he would certainly die there. He should absolutely return home with her. Kalu Rinpoche did not listen to her and assured her that he would not die, as he was dwelling in meditative absorption. It was useless for her to worry.

"Come back home with me for just a few days," she insisted. "We will load the horses and give you food and everything that you need. Later, if you want, you will be able to come back to your retreat. But do not stay here with nothing!"

"It is not necessary for me to go home," said the hermit. "I do not even need the food you have brought me. You can take it back with you."

"Please, at least keep this food."

"All right, I will keep it. But it will not be for me only," Kalu Rinpoche cheerfully replied. "I have many small companions with me here. They are ants. We are going to share. When you go back to the village, do not tell this to anyone. If you speak out, that would create obstacles to my retreat. People would want to bring me food and this would create disturbances. You can tell my father, but no one else."

Returning home, she told her husband what she had seen. He was not particularly surprised. "My son is in the stage of asceticism. To devote time to austerity is wonderful. We should not prevent him from doing so."

This answer hardly satisfied the mother, who yelled with anger, "Beautiful words are good, but meanwhile you are letting our son die! It would be better to have food delivered to him there!"

The father replied that if she was concerned for her child, the best thing she could do would be to accumulate a lot of merit. This would certainly be beneficial to the young meditator.

ONE OR SEVERAL?

Although Kalu Rinpoche had wished to keep his retreat secret, some animal breeders noticed that the cave was inhabited. First, they were not sure if it was inhabited by a madman or a lama. Approaching, they observed that it was a yogi. They began to visit him, bringing him tsampa,[14] curd, and other food. When they asked his name, he answered "My name is Karma." All the nomads discussed with admiration a certain "Lama Karma."

The disturbance, however, became too much and Kalu Rinpoche decided to look elsewhere for greater solitude. He traveled to a wooded area, and installed himself under a great tree. He wore no clothes and covered his body up to the neck

---

[14] Tsampa is a mixture of tea and roasted barley.

with a great heap of leaves.[15] He dwelled so long in retreat in this strange outfit that he created fear on the part of some people who no longer knew whether they were dealing with a man or a demonic creature. When asked his name, he replied, "My name is Lodro," using the name he received when taking the bodhisattva vows. The result was that people were now talking about "Lama Lodro."

Again, visitors became too numerous, so he left and went to a cave in which he had nothing besides three stones that he used as a stove to boil water, and a small quantity of tsampa. Yogis who meditate in caves generally do not enjoy a comfortable situation, but they at least have a minimum of commonly used objects. Kalu Rinpoche lived in complete destitution. Later, when Kalu Rinpoche founded retreat centers, he sometimes would hear retreatants complaining about dampness, smallness, or other defects of their cells. He would respond to the complainers, "You are right," but at the same time, he could not hold back a smile.

Another place he sometimes chose for his retreat was close to an elevated lake, accessible only in summer. He lived there several winters, and no one could bring him food. Each time he changed location, he also changed his name. In Kham,[16] some people were heard talking about the famous hermit called "Lama Karma"; others about the famous yogi, "Lama Lodro"; and others of the solitary meditator Lama so and so. No one suspected that it was the same person with different names.

---

[15]It is noted that later, following the death of Kalu Rinpoche, Situ Rinpoche was in charge of finding his new incarnation. He had a dream in which Kalu Rinpoche, covered with the leaves of trees, was flying in the space telling him, "I am Gyaltsen's son, I am Gyaltsen's son!"

[16] Kham is a region of Eastern Tibet.

It was a widespread belief that Kalu Rinpoche remained 12 years in solitary retreat, but Lama Gyaltsen thinks a more precise calculation is 15 years. To fulfill a request of Situ Rinpoche and Lama Norbu Tondrup, Kalu Rinpoche again started to be active in helping others by founding and supervising retreat centers. He also taught monks and laypeople, first in Kham, then elsewhere in Tibet.

MYSTERIOUS WORKERS

When Kalu Rinpoche, following Lama Norbu Tondrup, became retreat master of the center of Tsadra Rinchendra, he wanted to renovate and enlarge it. This project had already been envisioned by Jamgon Lodro Thaye, Situ Rinpoche, and Lama Norbu Tondrup himself. However, they had backed away from the project. The work was extremely difficult because of the presence of boulders, which seemingly hindered any new construction. Kalu Rinpoche said to Situ Rinpoche, who was in charge of Tsadra Rinchendra, "I know, you want to enlarge the retreat center. I am ready to take responsibility for this task. If you simply provide the necessary materials, I will manage the work."

"I do not believe this work is even possible," answered Situ Rinpoche.

"Yes, it is," insisted Kalu Rinpoche.

"And how will you do it?" asked Situ Rinpoche.

Then, Kalu Rinpoche presented a plan. He had drawn up the details for the future construction and was fully committed to accomplishing the work. Despite the fact they believed it was impossible, Situ Rinpoche and his counselors, facing the persistence of Kalu Rinpoche, agreed to provide materials and necessary workers. All those who had seen the plans would continue to believe that Kalu Rinpoche could not possibly undertake this project. Nevertheless, he told everybody not to worry. "We will do it," he assured everyone.

The laborers began to work hard, thinking that their efforts would be without result. They did not know they were going to benefit from mysterious helpers. Soon, they observed that each time they returned from a meal break or each time they resumed their task in the morning, some work had been done in their absence. What first appeared impossible to accomplish was finally finished. They noticed tracks of unusual size on the ground, marks left by four people who seemed to have been giants. Nevertheless, they saw no one. Everybody was amazed.

Kalu Rinpoche alone held the key to the mystery, from a dream he had. In this dream, a troop of tall and powerful men had come, holding in their hands spades, pickaxes, and other necessary tools for the construction.

"Where do you come from?" asked Kalu Rinpoche.

"We come from the monastery of the 'Accomplishing Wishes.'[17] We have heard that you wanted to accomplish a very difficult task. We are here to help you." Then they introduced themselves.

"I am Chetrapala" said one of them. "These are Zinamitra, Takiradza, and Dugon Trakshe."[18]

Thanks to the assistance of the invisible workers, the new buildings were constructed: 25 rooms for retreatants, a temple devoted to Six-Arm Mahakala, a temple devoted to the deity Chakrasamvara, the residence of the retreat master, a kitchen, a yoga hall, and so on.

---

[17]In Tibetan, Samdrup Gompa. In this case, it is not truly the name of a monastery, but an expression indicating that they could fulfill Kalu Rinpoche's wish.

[18]These four beings are four protectors from the retinue of the wrathful aspect deity, Six-Arm Mahakala (Chadrupa), who was Kalu Rinpoche's main protector.

Once, Kalu Rinpoche was invited to teach and give initiations in the two great Gelukpa monasteries of Sera and Drepung, near Lhasa. At Sera monastery, he was invited by two of the most eminent Gelukpa lamas, Mochok Rinpoche and Thome Rinpoche, and he gave empowerments to hundreds of monks.

During that time, traveling in the province of Tsang, he dreamed of three children coming to him. "I am Tsultrim Gonpo's Tulku,"[19] one of them said, "and these are two karmic friends. But now, I have met some obstacles."

"Do not worry about these obstacles," replied Kalu Rinpoche and, in the dream, he gave the child a skull cup and a knife.[20]

Some days later, continuing on his pilgrimage, he saw a village child playing. The child was similar to the one in his dream, and accompanied by the same two friends. The child seemed happy to see Kalu Rinpoche and spontaneously came to talk with him. This confirmed the feeling that Kalu Rinpoche had in his dream, and he knew then that he was in the presence of an exceptional child.

Somewhat later, Kalu Rinpoche went to Shangshung Dorjeden, a monastery founded by Khyungpo Naljor. The monastery had first belonged to the Shangpa lineage, and had later become a Gelukpa monastery. It had been supervised by a *geshe*[21] of Drepung, deceased for several years. The general secretary had expended great effort to discover the *geshe*'s reincarnation, but in vain. He was very old and tired. When Kalu Rinpoche came to visit him, the secretary told him, "You

---

[19]Tsultrim Gonpo was one of the past great lamas of the Shangpa lineage.

[20]Objects used in some Vajrayana rituals.

[21] *Geshe* literally means "spiritual friend." In the Gelugpa school, a *geshe* is a scholar who has completed a doctorate in traditional Buddhist studies.

are a representative of the Shangpa lineage. It is true that this monastery, now belonging to the Gelukpa lineage, was once the seat of the Shangpa lineage. I have not been able to find the reincarnation of our *geshe*, and I no longer have a lot of energy. Since you have arrived, I believe that it would be good to offer you this monastery. You take responsibility for it. I can no longer take care of it."

Kalu Rinpoche considered this a very happy set of circumstances. Announced by a dream, he had met Tsultrim Gonpo's Tulku, one of the past holders of the Shangpa lineage. Then the monastery, the lineage seat, was being offered to him. He decided to find the family of the child, which happened to be a rich family, and reveal what the dream had said. Although the family was of the Gelukpa lineage, the father and the mother had great confidence in Kalu Rinpoche, and they received the news that their son was a tulku with joy. Kalu Rinpoche suggested placing the child at the monastery of Shangshung Dorjeden[22] just given to him. It was agreed, and some time later, the child was led to the monastery and enthroned. Later, he received the totality of the Shangpa transmission from Kalu Rinpoche.

LAMA GYALTSEN'S MISSION

In the 1950s, although Kalu Rinpoche wished to go to Sikkim to hold a retreat, the Karmapa requested that he go to Bhutan. The Karmapa wanted the Dharma to recover all of its splendor in the country that had been strongly marked by the presence of Padmasambhava. Kalu Rinpoche took charge of a monastery in Bhutan for some time. Then he went to India

---

[22]During the Chinese invasion, Tsultrim Gonpo's monastery was destroyed. However, when the situation in Tibet became calmer, Tsultrim Gonpo was able to travel to India and meet Kalu Rinpoche in Sonada. Then, he returned to Tibet.

and founded several retreat centers in Dalhusy, in Tso Pema, in Madhya Pradesh, and finally in Sonada.

In the early 1960s, when no Tibetan lama had dreamed of teaching in the West, Kalu Rinpoche said jokingly, "I wonder if it would not be necessary to spread the Dharma in the country of the red-hair people," an expression by which Tibetans sometimes refer to Westerners, as they are noticeable in Asia by their reddish or blond hair. Sometimes it happened that Kalu Rinpoche's jokes were prophecies. Lama Gyaltsen asked. "Do you plan to go there?" "No, I am only joking," replied Kalu Rinpoche. However, the future would reveal that this joke was far from insignificant.

Indeed, a short while later, Kalu Rinpoche went to Rumtek[23] to see the Karmapa. During their meetings, they discussed the question of the possible introduction of the Dharma to the West. Their conclusion was that to have an exact idea of the situation there, it would be best to send someone to survey Western countries. Therefore, they asked Lama Gyaltsen if he would be willing to accept this role. He had begun to learn English in Darjeeling, but, aside from the rudiments of the language, he knew nothing of the distant countries of the "red-hair people." But, because his teachers were asking him, he accepted.

At this time, Tibetans had a blurred idea of the West. For them, because it was so far away, it was almost a mythical land from which no one returned. To go there was to disappear. When people close to Lama Gyaltsen knew he was getting ready for this great journey, they were astonished. What strange reason could persuade him to undertake such a crazy adventure? He simply replied that the only reason for his departure was the request made by Kalu Rinpoche and the Karmapa.

---

[23]Monastery in Sikkim where the Karmapa established his seat in exile.

In 1970, he flew first to England. Up to this point, he remembers, he did not feel entirely lost. From India, countries were next to each other. It was reassuring. America was more stressful. To go there, he had to cross an ocean that seemed limitless. Moreover, everything looked so strange, even the day was night and the night, day—compared with India.

Lama Gyaltsen stayed a year in the United States, visiting places as varied as New York, Texas, Minnesota, and Oklahoma. Zen Buddhism and Hinduism were taught a little, but not Tibetan Buddhism. Our "man with a mission" made many friends. Talking with people, he realized that not only did they have no idea of Tibetan culture, but sometimes they did not even know where Tibet was. He, especially, had begun to understand the Western paradox: a material comfort, unbelievable to an Easterner, accompanied by a strong inner discomfort. Many of his new friends had no religion, but he felt their need for something although their search was largely undefined. He explained concepts concerning the Buddha, Lama, Dharma, and so on. He particularly insisted on the notion that, according to Buddhism, all beings possess the seed of Buddhahood, the potential of becoming awakened, an idea that often provoked certain interest.

His observations led him to the following conclusion. It was probable that the Dharma of Tibet would be beneficial to the West because it seemed to answer some needs. However, it had to be taught by a realized lama. A scholar would risk transmitting nothing beneficial for the mind, and also lose his way.

The links of friendship forged by Lama Gyaltsen in America were very strong. Many people who served as his hosts considered him as their own son. They wanted to keep him with them and pay for his studies at a university. Despite the sadness created by his leaving, he decided to return to India. It was now necessary to report what he had found in his mission.

Back in India, he shared his impressions of traveling with the Karmapa and Kalu Rinpoche, emphasizing the fact that a lama who was only a scholar would be unable to efficiently bring the Dharma to the West. An accomplished lama was needed. After examining this issue, the Karmapa declared, "If Kalu Rinpoche can go to the West, he will certainly accomplish much benefit. He is a real bodhisattva and his realization is very great." Therefore, the Karmapa asked Kalu Rinpoche if he would accept the assignment.

"If it is a matter of benefitting beings, I am ready to go, even if I become ill or die," replied Kalu Rinpoche.

THE WEST: FOR AND AGAINST ALL

With the exception of Trungpa Rinpoche and Akong Rinpoche,[24] who were young and thoroughly trained in western culture, no Tibetan lama had ever taught in Europe or America. Most Tibetans wondered whether their tradition could interest Westerners as something other than a mere object of curiosity. When Kalu Rinpoche decided to go, a number of his compatriots wondered if the old lama had not simply lost his reason. They told him that he was already very old, that he knew neither the languages nor the customs of these distant countries, and that he would encounter immense difficulties.

As far as Kalu Rinpoche was concerned, he already had a few disciples from Europe or America, but he did not deny the extreme differences in lifestyle, culture, or manner of thinking that distinguished Tibetans from Westerners. Nevertheless, he profoundly believed that the mind was the same, not only as Buddha nature, but also in its aspiration for happiness and its wish to avoid the suffering engendered by the flow of conflicting emotions and karma that hold the mind

---

[24]Then installed in Scotland.

prisoner. The teachings of the Buddha function to liberate all beings, whoever they are, from their common prison. This is why Kalu Rinpoche was convinced that Tibetan Buddhism was more universal than just Tibetan and that Westerners could also find a spiritual nourishment within it.

Circumstances were favorable for Kalu Rinpoche's project. It happened at this time that a wealthy American disciple named James Ebin decided to invite Kalu Rinpoche to his country. Therefore, Kalu Rinpoche left India in 1971, going first in Jerusalem where he paid homage to holy places, then to Rome where he had an interview with Pope Paul VI, and finally to Paris where he stayed a few days with Anne Berry, his first French disciple. He spent a year in the United States and Canada, then returned to France.

Tibetans, as we have seen, hardly believed in the possibility of introducing the Dharma to the West, and they were not the only ones. During Kalu Rinpoche's first sojourn in Paris, a Frenchman who had some knowledge of Buddhism because he worked at the Burmese Embassy, and who later helped spread Tibetan Buddhism in France, came to see him at Anne Berry's home to express his point of view about this visit.

"We are happy you are in France, but above all, do not teach Buddhism! Here, everyone is a Christian and if you were to teach, no one would be interested. On the contrary, you would only make people uncomfortable. Do not hope to make the Dharma known here."

"Your viewpoint undoubtedly has certain value," replied Kalu Rinpoche. "However, Christian people practice religion. They believe in a superior reality, God, and they also believe that the consequences of their acts can lead them to heaven or hell. I, myself, have met with the Pope and felt great joy at this meeting. I have a great esteem for Christians, and I believe that they also would appreciate Buddhist teachings."

The man burst into laughter, showing his profound skepticism.

"Christianity and Buddhism have the same goal, which is to help all beings," added Kalu Rinpoche. "Both traditions share in preventing beings from falling into inferior worlds and in guiding beings toward liberation. They can understand each other, and I hope my teaching will be beneficial. I will go now to America," he concluded, "but I will return to France and teach. My sole wish is that everyone who sees me, hears about me, touches me, or thinks of me, who has a connection with me in one way or another, will obtain Buddhahood. This is why I believe that I can be useful."

After returning from America, Kalu Rinpoche was again invited to visit by Anne Berry. He taught in many places and had many disciples. Two or three years later, the skeptical Frenchman met him again and acknowledged his misjudgment. He had not believed it possible to teach Buddhism in France and interest people. He was surprised and expressed his admiration.

This first trip opened the gate to the teaching of Tibetan Buddhism in America and Europe. An anecdote may help us to appreciate this influence. In the USA, in the west coast city of Seattle, a Sakyapa lama of the same generation as Kalu Rinpoche made his residence. His name was Deshung Rinpoche. He was both a scholar and a realized being. American authorities had invited him to teach Tibetan language at their university. Conscientiously filling his duties, he noticed that his students were showing interest in Tibetan culture and civilization. However, he did not think that North Americans would become intimately involved in the Buddhist approach. How surprised he was one day to see a young American wearing a *mala* around his neck. He asked the American if he wore the *mala* as a necklace or if he used it. Yes, the young man used it. He had taken refuge, recited mantras, and had come to ask Deshung Rinpoche some precise questions. Who taught him all this? It was none other than Kalu Rinpoche. Deshung Rinpoche was impressed. From then on, he changed his thinking about Buddhism for Westerners. He began to teach and was followed by many disciples. He had not even imagined that they would be interested in a 1000-year-old doctrine coming from the Land of Snow!

Back in India, Kalu Rinpoche reported on his journey to the Karmapa and encouraged the Karmapa to go to the West. Because of his privileged relationship with many great lamas of other lineages, Kalu Rinpoche inspired the Dalai Lama (Gelukpa), Dilgo Khyentse Rinpoche, Dudjom Rinpoche (Nyingmapas), Sakya Trizin (Sakyapa), and others lamas by his own experience of teaching in these far-away countries.

SPONTANEOUS ESTEEM FOR CHRISTIANITY

After Jerusalem, the second stop made by Kalu Rinpoche in the West was Rome, where he obtained an interview with Pope Paul VI. This certainly was the first encounter between a Pope and a Tibetan Lama.

Lama Gyaltsen, who was present during the interview, retained vivid memories of it. First, Kalu Rinpoche introduced himself, explained the situation in Eastern Tibet, and stated the direction of his activity. "I try to benefit all beings."

As for the Pope, he talked about his preoccupations. "Nowadays, there are wars and great difficulties on the planet earth; this is because people do not keep the vows and commitments they have made. From that, there is misfortune and suffering in this world. I beg you to pray for people to respect their vows and commitments in order for harmony to reign throughout the world."

According to Lama Gyaltsen, happiness at this encounter was visible on the face of the head of Catholicism, as well as on the face of the Tibetan lama. Mutual understanding and appreciation appeared to be very profound. Kalu Rinpoche would later repeat that he was encouraged by the words of the Pope for his mission in the West.

Concerning this and other matters, the thought of Kalu Rinpoche always exceeded Tibetan norms. Generally, Tibetans had no interest in meeting representatives of other religions. Before his first journey, Kalu Rinpoche had said that, as far as he was concerned, he wanted to meet qualified representatives of Christianity. Other people found this quite strange. Why did a great lama want to have contact with Christians? "It is beneficial," replied Kalu Rinpoche.

In Kham, Kalu Rinpoche had already heard about Christianity from missionaries who were living there. They translated some Christian books into Tibetan; spoke about God, heaven, and hell; and they helped the poor. However, the purpose of the teaching was viewed differently by the missionaries and the lamas. Missionaries preached far and wide in order to convert people to Christianity. As for the lamas, they considered that if there was an aspiration by someone to become Buddhist, they would reply to it, otherwise they contented themselves with praying for the benefit of all beings. They did not think it was absolutely necessary to convert people to Buddhism. This desire of the missionaries to convert people hardly pleased Tibetans. For example, at Kandze Marathong, a town in Kham, missionaries had erected large buildings and the Khampas, insulted by the display of this conquering attitude, ended up burning down the buildings.

When he lived in Kham, Kalu Rinpoche had read some books translated by the missionaries. He was disappointed to discover the lack of profundity in them. They only described the good that leads to heaven and the sin that leads to hell. They contain no vision of ultimate reality or any equivalent to liberation or Buddhahood. This disappointment was far from being a judgment. From then on, Kalu Rinpoche used to say that Christianity was certainly an authentic tradition, but that the external presentation of it was, no doubt, a primary approach. As presented to him, its deeper aspects were not manifest.

Moved by the wish to know Christianity better and meet priests capable of revealing the profound meaning of their tradition, he wanted to visit holy places in Israel and meet with the Pope in Rome. Then, in America and Canada, he met many priests and ministers. A particularly interesting encounter took place with the help of M. Lalungpa, a Tibetan living in the United States who had a perfect command of the English language. Kalu Rinpoche asked questions of the Christians and answered their questions as well. Both the Christians and Kalu Rinpoche were happy with the answers to their questions. After this, Kalu Rinpoche often said that the Christian tradition appeared good to him, and that it was certainly capable of helping many people.

GIVING EVERYTHING AWAY

One of the practices of Tibetan lamas is to offer all their possessions to their master. Lama Gyaltsen witnessed this several times on behalf of Kalu Rinpoche. The manner in which Kalu Rinpoche dealt with such material donations is explained by Lama Gyaltsen. The response was sometimes surprising and disconcerting for people when it was not perfectly understood. Although Kalu Rinpoche never asked for anything, he never refused to teach, and never discriminated between the poor and the rich. He never refused an offering, and sometimes he gave the impression of accumulating. And it was true that he accumulated things for two or three years, giving donated money to Lama Gyaltsen, who was in charge of the money without being allowed to use it. When Kalu Rinpoche thought the sum in his possession was sufficient, he divided it into three uneven parts. The largest one, he offered to the Lama, and, in one way or another, to the Three Jewels. The second portion was reserved for the poor, and the third was devoted to the feeding of animals. In the end, he kept nothing for himself, being free of all attachment.

He was always satisfied. If someone gave him food, he did not request another kind. If he wore a piece of cloth, he did not wish to have another one and was concerned with neither cold nor heat. He could wear a heavy piece of clothing during the summer heat, and not request warm clothing during the cold season. He often wore clothes made of fine and beautiful fabrics. They were offered to him by his disciples and servants. He, himself, did not feel any need for them. In India, when a single mosquito seeks to sting, we do everything to chase it away; Kalu Rinpoche never budged when mosquitoes devoured his arm. In everything, he was extremely simple and completely detached.

Through these episodes of Kalu Rinpoche's life, we have some idea of the person. However, as far as knowing the extent of his beneficial activity and the profundity of his realization, we cannot. The activity of bodhisattvas is indeed so vast; it goes beyond our capability of understanding.

The First Karmapa, Tusum Kyenpa (1110-1193)

The Events of Kalu Rinpoche's Life

Bokar Rinpoche wrote this short biography just after Kalu Rinpoche passed away.

THE NURTURING OF FAITH

A Summary of the Awakened Activity of the Sublime Lama

OM SOTI
*With the majesty of countless aeons of the two accumulations, you
have nurtured your being,
You have gained the mastery of creation, completion, and bodhicitta
And enjoy the magnificent fulfillment of the two benefits, for self
and others
Rangjung Kunkhyab, Naturally-Arising and All-Pervading,
I prostrate at your feet.*

These words of eulogy introduce the account of the
glorious and holy Lama, a supreme guide, whose perfect
kindness and wonderful activity encompass all teachings and
beings in these times of degeneration. When it is necessary to
speak of him by name, he is called the Lord of Refuge,
Khyabje Kalu Rinpoche, the Lama Vajradhara. This brief
summary of the activity of this Awakened Lama is offered as
a reminder and incentive to nourish the faith of those who are
devoted to him. As many beings of great vision have attested,
he is the manifestation of Awakened activity of Jamgon
Kongtrul Lodro Thaye. Jamgon Kongtrul, whose life was
prophesied by the Buddha, was the light of the teachings of
all traditions and the crown ornament of all the learned and
accomplished ones in the Land of Snows (Tibet). The Lord of

Refuge, Lama Vajradhara, Khyabje Kalu Rinpoche, was born amid marvelous signs and portents in the chain of snowy mountains of Tresho in Kham, eastern Tibet, in the year 1904. His father, Lekshe Drayang, was a mantric adept, the thirteenth in the series of incarnations of Ratak Palsang; and Drolkar (White Tara) was his mother. Even from a very early age, he exhibited signs characteristic of a spiritually advanced being and indicative of prior training. These signs included renunciation of cyclic existence, compassion for beings, and faith and devotion toward lamas and the Dharma. He learned to read and write and developed an understanding of the meaning of the Dharma without any effort, simply by receiving these teachings.

During his thirteenth year, at the major Kagyu seat in eastern Tibet, the monastery of Palpung, he received monastic ordination from Jamgon Tai Situ Pema Wangchok and received the name Karma Rangjung Kunkhyab, Naturally-Arising and All-Pervading. The fact that his name and its significance were in perfect agreement was later recognized by all.

At the age of 16, he entered the great retreat center of Tsadra Rinchendrak, the seat of Jamgon Lodro Thaye, where he completed the retreat of three years and three months. At that time, he received ripening empowerments and liberating instructions of the old and new translation schools, and in particular, the instructions and practice techniques of the Five Golden Teachings of the great siddha Khyungpo Naljor. These he received directly from the retreat master, Lama Norbu Tondrub, who had brought his own experience and realization to perfection. All these teachings were bestowed and received, just as the full contents of one vase are poured into another. While cultivating the familiarization with and accomplishment of these practices, he exhibited unusually excellent faith, diligence, experience, and realization.

Both before and after this retreat, he studied, meditated on, and practiced innumerable cycles of ripening empowerments and liberating instructions connected with the sutras and tantras of the old and new translation schools. He received these teachings from many great beings of all traditions. These included the erudite Tashi Chopel, a disciple of Jamgon Kongtrul, Situ Pema Wangchok, Khyentse Shenpen Ozer, Palden Khyentse Ozer, Pawo Tsuklak Mawe Wangchuk, Tsatsa Drubgyu, Dzogchen Rinpoche, Zhechen Gyaltsap, Zhechen Kongtrul, and Khyentse Chokyi Lodro. Wishing to give up all the comforts and riches of this life and being satisfied with whatever was at hand, he dedicated himself exclusively, to nurturing the force of his heartfelt aspiration to practice meditation in a mountain retreat.

Consequently, at the age of 25, he renounced everything, externally and internally—companions, servants, family ties, material comfort, and so on. He lived in solitary mountain retreats at Lhapu, in the region of Derge, and in various other places. For 12 years, he practiced the strictest possible asceticism with indefatigable perseverance.

Subsequently, at the command of Situ Pema Wangchok, he returned to Palpung and served over a period of many years as the retreat master and lama of the two retreat centers, Naroling and Niguling. Of the numerous disciples who completed the retreat, bearing the victory banner of practice, many are still living today in eastern, central, and western Tibet. When he was 40, Kalu Rinpoche visited and made offerings before the Jowo and Sakyamuni, the two principal statues in Lhasa, and visited important places of pilgrimage in central and western Tibet. When in Lhasa, he bestowed the ripening empowerments, liberating instructions, and supportive scriptural transmissions for the Five Golden Teachings of the glorious Shangpa Kagyu to many beings, such as Kar Dorje from Sera Monastery, to Lhatsun Rinpoche, to Tokme Rinpoche, and to Mokchok Je of Drepung Monastery. In this way, he entrusted them with the teachings of the Shangpa Kagyu lineage.

Kalu Rinpoche revitalized the teachings of the Jonang and Shangpa traditions at such places as Taranata's monastery of Takten Puntsokling, the seat of the Jonang—a tradition enriched by the majesty of both its cultural and spiritual heritage. He fostered these systems of teachings at Khyungpo Naljor's monastery, the Vajra Seat of Zhang Zhun, and Mokchokpa's monasteries at Lhapu and Nyetang. Thus, he initiated great activity beneficial to both the doctrine and beings. After that, Rinpoche traveled to Eastern Tibet and resided in Palpung Monastery and Horkok. There he received teachings, which he contemplated, cultivated, and accomplished. He then propagated these through imparting empowerments, scriptural transmissions, and explanations. Rinpoche thus furthered the development of the teachings and brought significant benefit to all beings connected to him.

In 1955, because of the unsettled conditions in eastern Tibet, Rinpoche returned to central Tibet. Princess Ashe Wangmo of the Kingdom of Bhutan was a being who had developed noble aspirations and was of excellent character. Hearing of the fame of this great lama, she became extremely devoted to him. She fervently requested His Holiness, the supreme and glorious 16th Karmapa, to appoint Rinpoche as the abbot of Jangchub Choling Monastery in the Kurto region of Bhutan, and as the personal lama of the royal family. As a result, His Holiness issued a directive that Rinpoche should go to Bhutan, which he did in 1957. For many years, he maintained, protected, and propagated the teachings. He established new retreat centers for the teachings of both the Kamtsang and Shangpa traditions, and built new stupas. Through his activities in that region, Rinpoche led many disciples on the path to freedom and omniscience.

In 1966, Rinpoche moved to Samdrup Darjayling Monastery in Sonada, Darjeeling District, India. The first project that he carried out there was the building of a three-year retreat center. At Rumtek Monastery, in 1973, following the directive of His Holiness, the great 16th Karmapa, Kalu Rinpoche fully bestowed various cycles of teachings to the four Eminences who are the light of the Kagyu traditions—Shamar Rinpoche, Situ Rinpoche, Jamgon Rinpoche, and Gyaltsap Rinpoche. These teachings included instructions for the path of skillful means of the Karma Kamtsang practice lineage—the Six Doctrines of Naropa that derive from the tradition of the four transmissions—and the path of liberation, mahamudra. Moreover, he bestowed the complete cycle of the Five Golden Teachings of the Shangpa tradition. The entirety of these teachings was imparted and received just as the contents of one vase are poured into another.

Similarly, following the directive of His Holiness the Dalai Lama, Rinpoche bestowed empowerments and scriptural transmissions to many spiritual friends, such as abbots and lamas of His Holiness' own monastic college, Namgyal Tratsang, and to those of the upper and lower tantric colleges. Included were the Five Golden Teachings of the Shangpa tradition, the cycle of Thirteen Empowerments of the Protector, and Dorje Phurba of the New Treasure tradition.

From 1971 until 1981, Rinpoche traveled many times to various lands: the United States, Canada, Europe, Southeast Asia, and so on. Rinpoche nurtured those who became his disciples by first giving them the vow of refuge in the Three Jewels. He gave instructions in the paths of the Small and Great Vehicles, emphasizing the law of karma, the cultivation of virtue, and the elimination of unwholesome actions. In particular, he bestowed the ripening empowerments and liberating instructions of Vajrayana, and most significantly, he conferred the great empowerment of glorious Kalachakra many times. The principal way, however, that Rinpoche fostered the spiritual growth of his disciples was to impart full instructions in the meditation of the Great Compassionate One, Chenrezig. In various countries, Rinpoche established more than 70 Dharma centers and 20 retreat centers and built 20 stupas. Rinpoche entrusted the responsibility of these centers to more than 30 lamas who were his students and had completed the three-year retreat. His spiritual activity and extraordinary kindness toward beings had a tremendous influence on all beings throughout this world and gave the Buddhist teachings added impact.

In 1983, Rinpoche further manifested his great concern for others by bestowing the Treasury of Precious Revealed Instructions to the Crown Ornaments of the Kagyu tradition, Their Eminences, the Regents of His Holiness Karmapa.

In all, several thousand lamas, tulkus, members of the sangha, and faithful disciples from India, Tibet, Sikkim, Bhutan, and all parts of the world, both East and West, gathered to receive this cycle of essential instructions. Out of compassion toward all beings, Rinpoche resolved to further their understanding and practice of the three vehicles of the Buddha's sacred Dharma. Accordingly, in 1986, he established a translation group called "The International Translation Committee" for the translation of the Encyclopedia of Knowledge (the Great Treatise, All-Pervading Knowledge, the Condensation of the Ocean of Buddhist Sutras, Tantras, and Culture). Translators from various Western countries are presently continuing this work under the guidance of qualified Tibetan scholars of all traditions.

In 1988, Rinpoche began construction of a 100-foot stupa beside a major thoroughfare in Salugara, near Siliguri, West Bengal, in the eastern part of India. This stupa will hold five types of relics, and will be an object of veneration that will bring liberation to anyone who sees it.

In February of 1989, Kalu Rinpoche traveled to Sherab Ling, the seat of His Eminence, Situ Rinpoche. He joined Situ Rinpoche and other eminent Regents to preside over the ritual of Mahakala, to observe the sacred dances, and to participate in the elaborate festivities celebrating the new year.

From there, Kalu Rinpoche journeyed to Dharamsala to meet with His Holiness the Dalai Lama. At that time, His Holiness expressed his appreciation for Rinpoche's various activities in the interest of Buddhist teachings and all beings, and His Holiness offered his encouragement for these projects.

On the fifteenth of March, Kalu Rinpoche returned to his home, his monastery in Sonada. From then on, Rinpoche showed signs of increasing physical discomfort. His closest attendant, his nephew Lama Gyaltsen, felt unable to take the responsibility for Rinpoche's medical care upon himself. He therefore encouraged Rinpoche to travel to New Delhi, France, or another country in the East or West, to take advantage of superior medical facilities. Rinpoche, however, did not accept this suggestion, saying that wherever he might travel, it would ultimately be of no benefit to his health, and that it would be best to remain where he was. After that, Rinpoche's health deteriorated, and, following the advice of his doctor, he went to a nursing home in Siliguri to receive medical attention and stayed there for three weeks. At this point, his health showed signs of improvement.

On the fifth of May, Rinpoche returned to his monastery in Sonada. After a few days, however, his health again became critical. On the tenth of May, 1989, at 3:00 P.M., at the age of 85, this exemplary being appeared to have left his physical body. His mind, in the pure state of clear light, merged inseparably with the expanse of totality. He has put aside his physical manifestation in this world for a period, out of the noblest of intentions: to provide incentive for those who, like me, have become more untamed in spite of our connection with the Dharma and cling to notions of permanence, and out of consideration for beings in other realms in need of his influence.

All of us—his disciples, followers, and those in any way connected to him—were plunged into the darkness of despair, without refuge or protection. At that time of complete helplessness, Their Eminences Jamgon Kongtrul Rinpoche, Shamar Rinpoche, Chadral Rinpoche, Situ Rinpoche, Gyaltsap Rinpoche, and others arrived, in succession, and paid homage to the *ku dung*, Rinpoche's sacred remains.

They offered fervent prayers that the vision and noble intentions of Kalu Rinpoche might be fully and ultimately realized. Above all, they lightened our sorrow by giving us the firm assurance that a precious tulku will soon appear to become once again a protector of the teachings and a guide for all beings—myself and all his disciples and followers. To that end, they composed and gave us several prayers for his swift rebirth. Moreover, each presided over the rituals performed during the seven successive weeks and manifested uplifting care and kindness.

In summary, from a very early age, our Noble Lama developed a feeling of disinterest in worldly life, which led him to renounce cyclic existence and enter the gate of the Buddha's precious teaching. This great Vajra-Master came to hold the three types of ordination—the individual liberation vows, the bodhisattva vows, and the Vajrayana vows.

Through listening, reflecting, and meditating, he furthered his personal spiritual development. Through exposition, debate, and composition, he benefitted others. Through his qualities of intelligence, nobility, and integrity, he benefitted himself and others. Through the nine qualities characteristic of spiritually developed beings, he explained, propagated, maintained, and protected the teachings of the Conqueror, and most particularly, the precious teachings of the Karma Kagyu and Shangpa Kagyu traditions. Out of his exceptional kindness and bodhicitta, he furthered the propagation of these teachings by establishing communities of ordained sangha, the very foundation of the Buddhist doctrine, and by founding centers for the study and practice of the Dharma. He has carried out this activity throughout the world—in the central and wider regions of Tibet, in India, China, Bhutan, Sikkim, and so on. In these ways, he has been unequaled in enriching and extending the life of the sacred instructions. Among his numerous disciples who are lineage holders are many exceptional spiritual friends: the eminent Regents of the Kagyu tradition who are the spiritual sons of His Holiness Karmapa, as well as lamas and incarnate tulkus of all traditions. Moreover, in the world, there are countless people, both men and women, who have had the good fortune to be his disciples. And, there have been numberless beings who have had significant connection with him. He has placed all of them on the path to freedom and omniscience.

This brief account of the events of Rinpoche's life has been written by a disciple of the lowest capability, one who has enjoyed for many years the kind protection of this Noble Lama, Great Vajradhara himself. I, the one called Bokar Tulku or Karma Ngedon Chokyi Lodro, have composed this on the third of June, 1989, in front of the precious ku dung. By this, may I and all beings attain the state of realization of this Noble Lama. Sarva Mangalam.

White Tara

Kalu Rinpoche's Last Moments

What follows are two open letters addressed to all disciples of the Lord of Refuge, Khyabje Kalu Rinpoche, from Bokar Tulku Rinpoche, Rinpoche's principal disciple and Dharma heir, Lama Gyaltsen, Rinpoche's nephew and life-long personal attendant, and Khenpo Lodro Donyo, abbot of Sonada Monastery. These letters are in Bokar Rinpoche's handwriting, while the content represents their shared experience.

OPEN LETTERS TO DISCIPLES AND FRIENDS OF THE LORD OF REFUGE, KHYABJE KALU RINPOCHE

At 8 P.M., Wednesday, May 10, 1989, our precious Lama, Khyabje Kalu Rinpoche, passed from this world into the pure realms. In the interest of bringing Rinpoche's presence closer to each of his disciples at this time of our shared loss and grief, we would like to present an account of the events of the last few months, as well as of the events that will now unfold.

In late November, Rinpoche traveled with the lamas and monks of his monastery, and with the members of his translation committee, a total of about 100 persons, to Bero Khyentse Rinpoche's monastery in Bodhgaya. Rinpoche made it clear that he wanted everyone to travel together with him, and so the monastery drove in a caravan of two buses and two cars—Rinpoche surrounded by his monks and disciples—from Sonada to Bodhgaya. Having established the activities of the lamas, monks and the translators, Rinpoche traveled to Los Angeles for a visit of a few weeks, during which he gave a number of empowerments and teachings. Rinpoche was invited to stay in America to build up his strength, but he was determined to return to India to support the translation work that had been his principal concern for the last two years.

Upon returning to India, Rinpoche visited Bodhgaya briefly, encouraging his monks and translators in their activities and meeting with Dilgo Khyentse Rinpoche, who was completing a Drupchen (great ritual) at the Kagyu monastery; then he traveled to Sherab Ling, the monastery of Tai Situ Rinpoche. Kalu Rinpoche had been invited on many occasions to visit Sherab Ling and had been unable to go there in the past. He felt this trip would allow him to participate in the *losar* (Tibetan New Year) festivities with Situ Rinpoche at Sherab Ling, and also to visit His Holiness, the Dalai Lama, who was in residence in Dharamsala at the time. He stayed about one week at Sherab Ling.

While there, Rinpoche was able to visit His Holiness in Dharamsala. They had a long visit, shared a meal, and discussed a number of subjects. His Holiness expressed pleasure with Rinpoche's activities, promised to do whatever he could to further the work of Rinpoche's translation project, and showed his concern for Rinpoche's health by having his personal physician examine Rinpoche. His Holiness commented that of all the lamas working to spread the Dharma throughout the world, there was none whose activity and kindness were greater than that of Rinpoche.

Rinpoche returned to Bodhgaya and stayed for another two weeks before moving his lamas, monks, and translators back to the Darjeeling District on February 22, traveling together as before.

Since Kalu Rinpoche had embarked on the construction of a major stupa in Salugara, near Siliguri, he remained there with all of his monastery for a period of three weeks, during which time the lamas and monks worked on the painting of the relief sculpture adorning the enclosing wall and the making of 100,000 *tsa-tsa*s for the stupa's eventual consecration. The translators continued their work on the translation of Jamgon Kongtrul Lodro Thaye's Encyclopedia of Knowledge. During this time, Rinpoche spent several hours each day at the stupa site, personally supervising various projects. Throughout this period, Rinpoche's health remained good, his activity undiminished.

On March 21, Rinpoche moved his monastery back to Sonada. Over a period of several weeks, Rinpoche seemed to become weaker, although medical opinion was that he had no specific illness. Lama Gyaltsen, myself, and others in Rinpoche's entourage encouraged Rinpoche to travel to Singapore or France to take advantage of better conditions there, but Rinpoche steadfastly refused to travel at that time. It was difficult for Rinpoche to eat, and the weakening of his body continued. On April 15, Dr. Wangdi of Darjeeling insisted that Rinpoche enter a hospital in Siliguri. Rinpoche was visited in the hospital by many Rinpoches, including Chadral Rinpoche, a great Nyingma lama and close friend; Jamgon Kongtrul Rinpoche; Gyaltsap Rinpoche; and others. Rinpoche's health improved slightly while he was in the hospital, but he continued to refuse any suggestion that he seek medical help elsewhere. After two weeks, Rinpoche was determined to return to his monastery in Sonada. The doctor felt strongly that he should remain in the hospital another three weeks. Finally, at the encouragement of myself and Khenpo Donyo, he agreed to remain one more week before returning to Sonada.

Rinpoche arrived home late in the afternoon on Friday, May 5. He was obviously happy to be home as he was carried up to his house, seated in a sedan-chair carried on the shoulders of several of his lamas, smiling and waving to different people. Rinpoche remained in strict retreat except for a short period the morning following his arrival, when he received the traditional welcoming scarves from all the members of the monastery. He remained alert and engaged throughout, occasionally speaking to people and showing concern for their well-being.

During these few days, Rinpoche was in good spirits and his health seemed stable. Lama Gyaltsen noticed that, whenever Kalu Rinpoche was asked about his health, Rinpoche would respond that he was well. Even when there seemed to be some external sign of physical difficulty, Rinpoche apparently would feel no suffering. So it was during those days. When asked how he was, Rinpoche responded, "Day-time is the cultivation of the experience of illusion. Night-time is the cultivation of the experience of dream."

Lama Gyaltsen and I both felt that this was a statement of Rinpoche's own state of mind at this time.

On one occasion, Kalu Rinpoche told me that having lived 85 years, he felt his life had been full and complete. While ordinary persons are never satisfied with their lives, or crave to live indefinitely, Rinpoche had no such regrets. One concern he did express was the fact that the translation of the Encyclopedia of Knowledge had not yet been completed, that perhaps his efforts to establish the translation committee had begun too late. Khenpo Donyo and I assured him that the committee was well established, the work well underway. We both promised to see the project through to completion. Even if Rinpoche was unable to see its realization, the work would be finished and would bear Rinpoche's name.

At two in the morning of May 10, Rinpoche's condition deteriorated dramatically. Only later did we discover he had suffered a heart attack. When he left the hospital, the doctor said his lungs were only working at 40 percent of capacity and that this placed additional strain on his heart. Khenpo Donyo was sent immediately to Siliguri, three hours away, to call the doctor from the hospital. Another car was sent to Darjeeling to call Dr. Wangdi. Chadral Rinpoche was called from his nearby monastery, and Jamgon Kongtrul Rinpoche was called from Rumtek. Chadral Rinpoche and the doctors were able to arrive quickly. Kalu Rinpoche was encouraged to return to the hospital in Siliguri, but refused. He said doctors could be called, but he was not leaving the monastery. Later in the morning, all of us having insisted that he return to the hospital, he finally said we could do what we liked. Everything was prepared for the move, the luggage was in the cars, when Rinpoche indicated he wanted to rest a few moments in his inner room. As he moved into the inner room, he was in full control of his body.

In the inner room he was put on oxygen and given glucose intravenously. His bed was pulled out from the wall, and to Rinpoche's right were Lama Gyaltsen and Khenpo Donyo, to Rinpoche's left were myself and Chadral Rinpoche. At one point Rinpoche asked to sit upright. The doctor and nurse forbade him to do so. A short time later he again indicated he wanted to sit up, and again the doctor and nurse adamantly refused to allow this. Lama Gyaltsen felt terrible, but powerless to contradict the doctor. Then Rinpoche himself tried to sit up, and had difficulty doing so. Lama Gyaltsen, feeling that perhaps this was the time, and that not to sit up could create an obstacle for Rinpoche, supported Rinpoche's back as he sat up. Rinpoche wanted to sit absolutely straight, both saying this and indicating with a gesture of his hand. The doctor and nurse were upset by this, so Rinpoche relaxed his posture slightly. He nevertheless assumed meditation posture. Tears were flowing down our faces uncontrollably and our hearts were filled with anguish.

Rinpoche placed his hands in meditation posture, his open eyes gazed outward in meditation, and his lips moved softly. A profound feeling of peace and happiness settled upon all of us and spread within our minds. All present felt that the indescribable happiness filling us was the faintest reflection of what was pervading Rinpoche's mind. Lama Gyaltsen also felt a fleeting experience of profound sorrow characteristic of compassionate awareness of the suffering pervading cyclic existence. This was felt to be a gift of Rinpoche's awareness. Slowly Rinpoche's gaze and his eyelids lowered and his breath stopped. The doctor and nurse wanted to try some extraordinary means to revive the breath, but Chadral Rinpoche indicated that Rinpoche should be left resting peacefully.

I have witnessed a number of people passing from this world. Occasionally there is a short rasping breath, occasionally a long inhalation or exhalation. With Rinpoche, there was none of these, but a most extraordinary passing into profound meditation.

The doctor performed his examination and then Chadral Rinpoche and I arranged his clothing and left him in his *tuk dam*, the Lama's final meditation. The environment was to be kept quiet, and Rinpoche not disturbed as long as the *tuk dam* lasted. An hour or two later, Jamgon Kongtrul Rinpoche arrived and spent a short time with Rinpoche. Both remarked how vital Rinpoche's form was, as though any moment he might begin to speak. The morning of the third day, Saturday, May 13, all the signs indicating that the *tuk dam* was complete had appeared. As we washed Rinpoche's body and changed his clothes, there were none of the usual traces of body waste or impurity. Also, the body remained soft and flexible, without any stiffness whatsoever. Rinpoche's body, now called *ku dung*, was placed in a prepared case covered with brocade and resides in Rinpoche's audience room.

In consultation with Jamgon Kongtrul Rinpoche and Chadral Rinpoche, the decision has been made not to cremate the *ku dung*, but to prepare it as a *mar dung*, so that it will always be with us. This was a tradition practiced in Tibet. In this way, the physical aspect of the Lama's form remains as a relic, a basis for religious inspiration. The Lama's activity continues as beings are liberated through seeing, hearing, considering, touching, or praising the relic of his *mar dung*. It is said that any connection whatsoever becomes beneficial, whether the mind of the being is positively inclined or not. In this way, the *mar dung* becomes the basis for the propagation and longevity of the teachings, the basis for both temporal and ultimate benefit of beings.

The departure of Khyabje Kalu Rinpoche from this world is a moment of extraordinary sadness for all sentient beings. The world has become a darker, poorer place because of his absence. His gentleness, the pervasiveness of his kindness, the brilliance of his wisdom, and the irresistibility of his sense of humor touched hearts in every part of the world. The subtlety of his insight and his total mastery of mind and phenomena are beyond the grasp of our ordinary understanding. It is difficult to fathom our extraordinary good fortune to have met and established a Dharma connection with such an Awakened being. Now there is no avoiding a feeling of profound personal sorrow at our loss.

Through Rinpoche's teaching, however, and our understanding of the Dharma, we know that all composite phenomena are impermanent, and that where we truly meet our Lama is in the ultimate openness of mind. The Lama is never separated from us, and never will be separate from us. What remains for us to do is to be true to Rinpoche's vision, his example, his teaching, and advice. This we can do through shedding our sorrow and celebrating the gifts of immeasurable kindness he has given us, through maintaining the purity of our commitments and our vajra bonds, through cultivating the qualities of an Awakened being that Rinpoche so clearly demonstrated to us. We should do this with the deepest prayers to Rinpoche that he quickly take human form, and return again to be with us.

With sincere best wishes to you all,

Bokar Tulku Rinpoche
Lama Gyaltsen
Khenpo Lodro Donyo

Sonada Monastery, May 15, 1989

ༀ་མུ་ནི།

Shakyamuni Buddha

The Story of His Reincarnation

The seven seas the dolphins roam
May drain from time and waves,
But Buddha's activity to guide his children
Will never be erased.

As this quote from the sutras indicates, it is the nature of spiritually advanced bodhisattvas to feel neither weary nor disheartened in their task of guiding those under their care, those in the endless and measureless realms of beings. These bodhisattvas aspire to uphold, nurture, and further the precious teachings of the Buddha, the source of comfort and joy in this world. Once they have donned the armor of this aspiration, they never waver in their goal. In response to the needs of others they produce delightful manifestations in a steady stream until the end of time. Their acts in service to Buddhism and for feeding the entire world will prove to be of lasting benefit.

An example of this can be found here among us, in the arrival of the reincarnation of the supreme manifestation of Awakening, our fearless guide, our omni-present spiritual master, Buddha Vajradhara incarnate, Kyabje (Lord of Refuge) Kalu Rinpoche. His return represents for us, his students in particular, and for the countless beings of this world, and for the boundless range of the teachings of the Buddha, a glorious flourishing of our merit. The following short account will describe his return among us.

A few years before Kalu Rinpoche's previous incarnation passed away to the realm of perfect peace, he told a group of disciples, "When I die, it will not be a dog's death. I will go having prepared every last detail."

On another occasion a patron who had faith in Rinpoche asked him, "Rinpoche, although you have now reached an advanced age, please allow your lotus feet to remain in this world. But when you cannot stay any longer, do not let your compassion grow faint. Please return in a supreme manifestation of Awakening to serve Buddhism and humanity in the future!"

In reply, Rinpoche said jokingly, "If you need my new incarnation, ask Gyaltsen."

Later, in his final years, Rinpoche ate only a tiny amount of food. Lama Gyaltsen begged him to eat more, but Rinpoche said in jest, "Why should I? When you are old and I am urging you to eat more, then you will understand!"

Furthermore, in his will, composed in 1976, Rinpoche bequeathed all he owned—particularly his principal monastic seat at Sonada, India, and his other monasteries and Buddhist meditation centers in India and in foreign countries—to Lama Gyaltsen Ratak.

If we examine these and other examples, it is evident that even from that time Rinpoche had decided to return in a supreme reincarnation of manifest Awakening and that he had foreseen details of his future life, such as the identity of his parents. As clearly related above, he had also made definite verbal predictions of those events: how could we have failed to understand the true meaning of his words? All of us have fallen under the pervasive power of habitual, mistaken thinking. Our faith, respect, and pure appreciation of our spiritual master and guide are as limited as a glimpse of him through a slit in a blindfold. Our aberrant view of him was as an ordinary companion no different from ourselves. Therefore, how could we have understood?

The Awakened qualities of this master's mind were especially profound and vast. It was difficult for anyone to plumb their breadth and depths. Now, with the benefit of hindsight, it is obvious that in whatever he did within the spiritual and worldly spheres of life, he acted with complete personal integrity. His acts did not contravene social norms, yet were in perfect harmony with the ways of spiritual life. His impeccable honesty prevented him from being unduly influenced by patrons or by other powerful individuals. He kept his own counsel entirely. In particular, he exercised complete mastery of his mind in the two forms of the precious mind of Awakening, and so dedicated his life to providing material and spiritual aid impartially to any person who needed them. His dedication was reinforced by his main spiritual practices: training in the mind of Awakening and the Aspirations of the Bodhisattva Samantabhadra, which include the Seven-Branch prayer. All phenomena—sights, sounds, or thoughts—were without reality for him, like the illusion of a dream. He remarked that for him everything became part of that experience. In everything he undertook, this master never acted on the basis of hopeful anticipation or fearful apprehension, and never made choices based on his own desires. To the depth of his being, he was content with whatever came his way.

In brief, this reincarnation, which has appeared so soon after his physical form dissolved into the ultimate realm of reality, represents the timely ripening of the fruit of his life devoted entirely to prayer and to the aspiration to serve Buddhism and all beings. He has been reborn as a descendent of the Ratak clan, whose members have included the majestic victor, the Karmapa Dusum Kyenpa, and many other great meditation masters. The father of this new incarnation is named Lama Gyaltsen, his close attendant and nephew during his former life. His mother is named Kalzang Drolkar, from

Kurlo in the Southern Kingdom of Bhutan.[25] In the midst of many wonderful dream-signs appearing to both parents during the pregnancy, this supreme manifestation of Awakening intentionally reentered the world. During the monthly fulfillment offerings to the Six-Arm Mahakala on September 17, 1990 (the twenty-ninth day of the eighth lunar month of the Iron Horse year), the flower of his perfect form first blossomed in Darjeeling, India. He was born without any harm to his mother. Even at that time, some faithful patrons of his previous incarnation felt unusually joyful, both physically and mentally, simply upon seeing the child's face. His monastery at Sonada was covered with a canopy of rainbow clouds and a number of significant, wonderful, and wholly positive signs appeared. From that moment on, people near and far spread the news, "The supreme reincarnation of our spiritual master has been born!"

As the child grew with the days and months, his character revealed itself to be peaceful, disciplined, and completely fearless. His greatest joy was found in playing the various ritual musical instruments, such as *radung* (long horns) and *gyaling* (short horns). This provides but one example of the fact that he acted naturally in ways that surpassed the behavior of ordinary children. Genuine indications of being a truly spiritual person who had previously cultivated the path were very clearly evident to all who met him.

During this period, the Lord of Refuge, the protector Loving-Kindness incarnate, Tai Situ Rinpoche, saw convincing signs that this child was indeed the supreme reincarnation of the previous Kyabje Kalu Rinpoche. However, Tai Situpa

---

[25]Kalzang Drolkar's father is Lama Ngawang Pekar from the Lamaykar lineage, a highly respected Dharma family. Before Kyabje Kalu Rinpoche arrived in Bhutan at Jangchub Choling, he was the spiritual director of the monastery appointed by the Bhutanese Princess Ashe Wangmo; after he became Rinpoche's disciple and served the monastery until he passed away at the age of 63.

insisted that the supreme head of the Buddha's teachings, His Holiness the Dalai Lama, be consulted to consider this candidate through his omniscient vision. Accordingly, this supreme refuge and protector confirmed that in the domain of his pure wisdom, the child, then one-and-a-half years old, was surely and unmistakenly the reincarnation of Kalu Rinpoche. On the auspicious day His Holiness' decree was received at the residence of the former Kalu Rinpoche, the monastery called Samdrup Darjay Choling at Sonada, Darjeeling, India. We, the abbot, disciples, and monks together, first performed a purification and washing ceremony for the new incarnation, then offered him robes, a name, and the representations of the Buddha's body, speech, and mind. Following this, ordained and laypeople came to meet him, led by the monks of this monastery.

In July 1992, the new incarnation was invited to visit the Buddhist meditation centers founded by his previous incarnation in France. During this tour, his disciples and many other people who met him were amazed and moved to faith by his presence.

In December 1992, he made his first pilgrimage to the supreme sacred place, the Vajra Seal (Bodhgaya in north-central India). Although still very small, he daily attended the great gathering to recite The Aspirations of the Bodhisattva Samantabhadra. While sitting at the head of the assembly, he played the ritual hand drum and bell proficiently. While in Bodhgaya, he prostrated and made offerings to the representations of the Buddha's body, speech, and mind, and gave gifts to the beggars there without having been taught to do so. His natural pleasure in doing these acts astonished everyone and led them automatically to have faith in him.

On February 25, 1993 (the fourth day of the first lunar month of the Water Bird year), the monastic seat of Samdrup Darjay Choling will be blessed by the kind visit of our supreme refuge and protector, His Holiness the Dalai Lama. On this occasion, His Holiness will graciously cut the topmost strands of the supreme reincarnation's hair, bestow a name, and give him his blessing. Following that, spiritual masters, reincarnate masters, and members of the spiritual communities of monasteries from all schools of Tibetan Buddhism; spiritual teachers representing Buddhist meditation centers in the West and Asia; Buddhist ordained and lay people, and members of the public will participate in the profound and complete ceremony of investiture and enthronement of this new incarnation.

This account has been written by Kalu Rinpoche's respectful servant, the one known by the name of Bokar Tulku, who lives within the cooling shadow of this protector's compassion. These words are accompanied by the request, prayer, and wish that the lotus feet of the three secret expressions—the body, speech, and mind—of this new incarnation of our illustrious, supreme spiritual master should remain upon his indestructible vajra throne for countless aeons, and that upon completion of his study, reflection, and meditation, his Awakened activity should reach the limits of the earth in emulation of the Awakened life of his predecessor.

Translated at Samdrup Darjay Choling Monastery, Sonada, India, by Kalu Rinpoche's International Translation Committee for Buddhist Texts.

Contribution of the Dharma to the World

I am an Easterner, as are the people who accompany me. You who listen to me this evening are Westerners. Despite this geographical difference, we are here together to approach the subject of the Dharma in daily life, because of karmic connections established in our past lives and our aspirations.

Sometimes East and West are considered two very different worlds. People, languages, and cultures appear to be separated by impassable borders. Nevertheless, one cannot draw such sharp lines between them. Easterners and Westerners share the same experience of human existence, through the supports of body, speech, and mind. Differences in customs and behavior are not fundamental.

To whichever civilization one refers, one always encounters the two aspects of temporal and spiritual life. The first aspect deals with the needs of this existence and seeks to improve material conditions. The second aims to maintain peace and happiness of the mind for this existence and beyond, leading to superior worlds and liberation.

PEACE IN THE WORLD, PEACE IN THE HEART

Beings live in numerous conditions of existence, which can be divided into inferior and superior worlds. The inferior worlds are characterized by great suffering felt during long periods of time. The superior worlds are not completely lacking in suffering, but they know some degrees of happiness. Human beings like us dwell in the first of these superior worlds.

Within the framework of human life, two things are important; the establishment of outer peace and happiness, and the establishment of inner peace and happiness. From an external point of view, right up to the greatest level, happiness depends on the relationships between nations. If they get along, seeking not to harm, but help each other, citizens enjoy peace and favorable conditions in life. Inside a country, the relationship between leaders and the people is another important factor. If leaders avoid quarrels and create harmony, acting in the interest of the people they govern and if the people respect their leaders, that will bring forth a happy situation.

Nevertheless, the most important domain for the external conditions of life to be favorable to happiness is the family. Harmony between parents and children, between husband and wife, between brothers and sisters, is essential.

FRATERNAL TRADITIONS

Religion is another element of the social fabric. There are numerous religions, and the Buddha had predicted the multiplicity of religious beliefs to follow him, while underlining the point that they were all rays of light of the same awakened activity benefitting beings according to their capacities and mentalities. This is why religions and spiritual traditions have to maintain fraternal relationships, never quarrelling, criticizing, or condemning each other.

The diversity of spiritual traditions is explained by the diversity of cultures and individual modes of thinking. Traditions try to bring an adequate answer to each context. Though having apparent differences, at least all the religions have the goal of avoiding conditions of inferior existence. According to the capacities of the beings, these traditions allow birth as a human being or in the divine worlds of the gods—in the sphere of desire, form, or formlessness—which, while remaining in samsara, provide beings with a happy and long existence. At best, traditions lead beyond samsara, to individual liberation which Buddhists call the states of *shravaka*, *arhat*, or *pratyeka* Buddha, or to the complete Awakening, Buddhahood. It depends on the capacity of the disciples.

All traditions share the same goal, which is to guide beings toward some states of superior existence. However, conflicts, and even wars, are present within these traditions. The cause does not have to be attributed to the traditions themselves, but to the people who represent them, as they are sometimes moved by conflicting emotions instead of spiritual convictions. If the nations could establish harmonious relationships and if different social groups within a country could do the same, followed by the members of the same family, the situation on earth would be happy. No war, no conflict, no starvation could exist.

NOBLE MIND, VILE MIND

In the political and social world, as well as in the domain of spiritual traditions, one encounters some people with noble motivations, others with base preoccupations. The predominance of one or the other constitutes an essential factor of progress or degeneration. A Tibetan saying is, "One recognizes countries by their language. One recognizes noble or vile people by their behavior." What type of behavior would allow us to distinguish the two categories of people? Let us suppose that a "noble mind" travels in the company of a "vile mind," through an arid region, in overwhelming heat. Both of them are tormented by thirst when they arrive at a place where there is a glass of water. The "noble person" arriving first will drink half of the glass of water, thinking that his or her companion arriving later, will also need to quench his or her thirst. If the "vile person" comes first, the glass of water will be swallowed at once without concern for anyone else.

Having a good heart, being concerned not only with oneself but also with others, is very important in the temporal domain as well as the spiritual one.

From a spiritual point of view, one is drawn to the teaching that others are more important than oneself. It is difficult to apply this principle to the rules of temporal life, but at least, it is possible to wish for others what one wishes for oneself, "If I need what is good and pleasant, then others do too." This type of egalitarian vision can only be beneficial.

WHO GOVERNS?

The happiness and misfortune of the world depend essentially on the minds of people. Body and speech are only the means of obeying the orders of the king, that is the mind. If the mind leans toward what is right, body and speech will be in the service of righteousness. If the mind is oriented toward evil, body and speech will be in the service of evil.

We are ordinary beings and we have little control of our own mind, which is placed under the direction of three elements:

- karmic tendencies inherited from past lives
- conflicting emotions
- discursive thinking

The mind has hardly more freedom than that of a small baby.

In order for it to grow, mature, and gain more freedom, it is necessary to meditate or, at least, to develop a good knowledge of the temporal and spiritual domains.

GREED AND CONTENTMENT

Buddhism divides the totality of possible existences into six classes, which are themselves divided in three spheres: the sphere of desire, the sphere of form, and the sphere of formlessness. Human beings belong to the sphere of desire. That is why desire and attachment are so restraining for them.

From this point, greed travels in two directions, toward oneself and toward others.

Greed toward oneself manifests in the desire to have one's own belongings; once they are obtained, strong feelings of ownership arise. "It is my house, these are my belongings, it is my family." Greed toward others is based on others' belongings. "They have a beautiful house, a beautiful car, and so on. I need to get the same!"

In its turn, greed is followed by many other complications, such as jealousy, pride, possessiveness, aggressiveness, hatred, and so on. Together they produce innumerable problems and lead us to commit negative acts. It is necessary for us to find the remedy for greed.

This remedy is contentment, the capability to be satisfied by what we have, and thinking, "This is enough for me, I am happy with what I have." Contentment is as useful a quality for the wealthy as for those who are not. Thanks to contentment, there are poor people who think, "I have enough to eat and to wear, I am happy. If I cannot acquire more, it is without doubt because of my past karma." As for the wealthy, they learn to not always want more, and particularly to not constantly look at others who possess more than they do. Through contentment, jealousy, pride, and many other defects spontaneously disappear. The Buddha said, "Contentment is the greatest of all treasures. No wealth can compete with it."

THE WEALTH OF THE SERVANT

In Tibet, one tells the story of a merchant who possessed a hundred dzos,[26] each carrying a load of tea. He had a worker to whom he gave one third of a load. This worker had no great needs. Without really knowing what to do with this tea, he thought that it was sufficient. Always cheerful, never

---

[26]The dzo is the offspring resulting from breeding a yak with a cow.

missing an opportunity to laugh, he had happy days. On the other hand, the merchant always worried. Concerned about losing his possessions, and greedy to acquire more, day and night, he was always planning to increase his business. Finally, the servant thought, "My poor master is always anxious. A hundred loads of tea do not make him happy, he always thinks of getting more. As for me, I have all I need to eat and dress myself. I am happy like that. I really do not need my share of tea. It would be better to give it to my master. Perhaps he will feel better."

He went to find his master and told him, "Do not be so anxious. Do you need more tea? Here, I give you mine."

This servant is an example of contentment. Satisfied with his situation, he is always happy!

INFINITE DISSATISFACTION

Contentment teaches us to be satisfied with what we have. In reality, we do not have the choice to do otherwise. Indeed, the mind is empty. Nothing can ever fill it. This is why dissatisfaction is limitless. The person who possesses $100,000 and is not content wants $200,000, but this will not satisfy the mind. The person who possesses a million and is not content wants 2 million, then 3, 4, 5 million, but the mind is never fulfilled.

This principle is not limited to material goods, but also pertains to human relationships. A man living with a woman with whom he is happy will nevertheless desire to have a relationship with another, then with a third one, and so on, if he his not content. This has consequences with multiple complications, suffering and quarrels. On the other hand, while living with a companion in what one considers to be a satisfactory relationship, life automatically becomes easy and pleasant.

In any situation, it is necessary to master our mind. If we allow it to follow its fantasies, we are sure to face many problems.

Let us suppose a husband becomes angry with his wife, or a wife with her husband. If one of them reacts with patience, anger will cease by itself. In order to practice patience, it is necessary to be the master of our own mind. If we answer violent words by violent words, anger will spread like fire. Fire will not extinguish fire. It is important to know how to control one's own mind.

A BED OF FLOWERS OR A BED OF THORNS

From the point of view of scenic beauty, houses, and material goods, the West resembles the world of gods. Nevertheless, people's minds seem to experience a lot of suffering. Why? Because, when conflicting emotions arise, one never seeks a remedy, but allows oneself to be carried away by the power of the conflicting emotions. When the mind is at peace, free of anger or any other conflicting emotion, a person is like someone lying on a bed of flowers. For the person full of anger or aggressiveness, it is like lying on a bed of thorns—each movement is painful.

At the moment, the world is under threat of many wars. These wars have no source other than conflicting emotions. Each country possesses land, goods, and wealth. Nevertheless, it happens that a country, wishing to grasp the wealth of a neighboring country, invades it. Where does the war come from in this case? It comes from desire. It can also happen that a country is simply jealous of the superior living style of another and, because of that, decides to go to war. Or again, pure hatred can motivate armed conflict. Whatever it is, desire, jealousy, or hatred, the source of war is not found anywhere other than in the conflicting emotions agitating people's minds. If conflicting emotions disappear, peace generates itself.

HUMAN BEINGS AND GODS

In several sutras, the Buddha expounded that human acts have consequences for the general harmony of the universe. When human beings let themselves be violently carried away by anger, aggressiveness, and conflicts, this encourages the demi-gods (Sanskrit, *asuras*) to attack the gods (Sanskrit, *devas*). When demi-gods achieve victory, the result is that wars, famines, epidemics, and other catastrophes occur on earth. When the gods are victorious, peace returns to the earth. Furthermore, the victory of demi-gods is sustained by negative acts accomplished by human beings, while the victory of the gods is sustained by positive human actions. Consequently, the person who reduces his or her conflicting emotions and negative acts automatically contributes to peace and general harmony.

TIBET, A SIMPLE COUNTRY

Tibet was a particularly fortunate country, because it received the complete transmission of the Buddha's teachings from India. Translators and scholars, working in collaboration with Indian scholars, have translated the totality of sutras and tantras into Tibetan, with the result that the Buddhist tradition was completely integrated with Tibetan civilization. The Tibet of the past did not resemble, in any way, the West of today. It was an unpolished and simple country where people had enough to eat and cloth themselves. Temporal activities were not very developed, and that left a lot of free time and energy for practice of the Dharma. The faith and diligence of Tibetans are great and, because of that, Buddhism has known, in their country, an extraordinary blossoming that remains to this day. Tibetan tradition has now spread throughout the entire world. There are several reasons for this.

THE WEST, A FERTILE SOIL

First of all, the Dharma is in itself very precious and beneficial. It can be received only by those who are the right vessel, and who have prepared themselves in their past lives by some purification and accumulation of merit. These are the people who are now interested in Buddhism in all the parts of the world.

A second factor favoring the introduction of Buddhism is constituted by the values taught by Christianity, certainly the most powerful religion on earth. Within Christianity, one meets the notion of a superior reality in the form of God and, therefore, the ideas of faith and prayer. One also finds there a strong emphasis on loving all human beings. From this love, generosity can be generated. Ethics, in this context, rejects negative conduct in favor of positive conduct.

These values are shared with Buddhism in this form and another. Therefore, Buddhism can be easily understood in a Christian context.

Third, most Westerners receive elaborate intellectual training, which allows them to approach and appreciate the profound and vast concepts proposed by Buddhism without difficulty. Finally, one considers that in the immensity of their compassion, Buddhas and bodhisattvas spontaneously produce an answer each time beings need help. This is why such great masters as the Dalai Lama, the Karmapa, and many others visit numerous countries in order to turn the Wheel of the Dharma.[27] All of these reasons explain the spread of the Dharma in the West.

SPIRITUAL AND TEMPORAL LIFE

Some people think the Dharma is on one side and ordinary life on the other, that they are separate. However, the Dharma

---

[27]Expression equivalent to giving the teaching of the Buddha.

and temporal life sustain each other. Without temporal support, the Dharma cannot be sustained. Thanks to the Dharma, the world enjoys a certain peace and happiness, and at the same time people can prepare for rebirth in superior worlds, and begin the path to liberation.

THREE LIFESTYLES

The Dharma itself can be approached in three ways.

In the first, one completely abandons any concern for this life and ordinary activity; one then goes to a hermitage to be exclusively devoted to meditation. This is following the example of Milarepa, who, in this manner, was able to obtain realization in one lifetime. Doing this is extraordinary.

Atisha and Gampopa provide us with perfect examples of the second approach which consists of adopting the life of a monk, observing the 253 vows that characterize it, and teaching the Dharma.

The third way is to remain in the world, to continue temporal work while developing faith, compassion, knowledge, and generosity, and by practicing the Dharma with ardor. The most beautiful examples of this lifestyle are found in people such as King Indraboddhi of India, the Tibetan kings Songtsen Gampo and Trisong Detsen, and Marpa the Translator.

Whatever mode of practice we choose, we must deal with the problem of conflicting emotions, whether by rejecting them, transforming them, or recognizing their essence.[28] If someone cannot devote a lot of time to the formal practice of the Dharma, has many worldly preoccupations, and needs a method to reduce the emotions, he or she will find this a great help. It will make life easier and much suffering will be

---

[28]These three ways to deal with conflicting emotions are described in detail in Volume Two, *Profound Buddhism*.

avoided. On the contrary, the situation of people who have no spiritual path is a very difficult one. They cling to the strong notion of "me" as a definite reality. They give the same reality to desire, anger, or other emotions, thinking that these truly exist by themselves. They cannot avoid submitting to their power.

EMOTIONS ARE EMPTY

Conflicting emotions, as well as the notion of "me," come from the mind which, in itself, has no form, color, or shape. It is, therefore, empty. Since the mind is empty, the emotions that it produces are also empty. When one recognizes their empty nature, their power disappears.

When an emotion arises, it arises from an empty mind. When the emotion is present, it stays empty in essence; when the emotion disappears, it reabsorbs itself in the empty mind. You can go to the seashore and look at the play of waves which rise, sometimes becoming immense. When the wave forms, it is nothing other than the water of the sea; when it is reabsorbed, it goes back to the water of the sea. In a similar manner, conflicting emotions are always part of the emptiness of the mind. They come from this emptiness, their essence is emptiness, they return to emptiness. They do not truly exist by themselves.

If we understand the nature of emotions, it is then easy to retain mastery of our minds. If we were animals, all that we have said this evening would be useless and beyond any possibility of comprehension. Since we are human beings, we have the ability to understand; we realize that we wish peace and happiness for this life and for our lives to come.

Then Kalu Rinpoche allowed a question-and-answer session.
Question: If the mind is empty, are the physical actions directed by the mind empty also?

Kalu Rinpoche: In truth, our acts are also empty, because all outer or inner phenomena are empty, stemming from emptiness of the mind. We can understand this by referring to our dreams. In them appear landscapes, houses, famous people, all kinds of things that exist nowhere other than in the mind. It is the same for every manifestation. It also explains the miraculous powers great yogis have over matter.

MILAREPA PARTICIPATES IN A POWER CONTEST

Once, Milarepa went to the shore of a lake not far from Mount Kailash, where a Bonpo yogi called Naro Penchung resided. The latter had obtained magical powers without having reached the realization of the empty nature of all phenomena; he was very proud of these powers. Naro Penchung was not very happy when Milarepa, whose reputation was very great, came to live in the same region and overshadowed him. He went to talk to Milarepa. "Your fame is great and I would like to challenge you in a power contest. If you are victorious, the region will be yours. If I win, the territory will be mine." Milarepa agreed.

To demonstrate his powers, Naro Penchung put one foot on the shore of the lake and, enormously expanding his body, placed his other foot on the other shore. As for Milarepa, he laid down on the lake. His body did not become larger and the lake did not become smaller. His body covered the complete surface of the lake. This was possible only because Milarepa had the realization of the empty nature of the phenomena.

Naro Penchung requested a second contest. He proposed that the two competitors leave an imprint of their hand or foot on the cliff overhanging the opposite shore of the lake. Lengthening his leg as much as he could, Naro Penchung could not exceed half of the lake's length in that direction. Milarepa simply raised his hand and an imprint immediately appeared on the cliff.

Naro Penchung did not accept failure. He requested a definitive test. The first one to arrive at the top of Mount Kailash the following morning would be victorious. At dawn, the next day, he sat on his magical drum and, beating it with all his energy, he quickly began to climb the mountain. Meanwhile, Milarepa did not move. He apparently did not prepare to begin his ascent and did not even watch the progress of his competitor. The disciples who accompanied him began to become anxious. Was their master going to lose?

Milarepa told them not to worry. From time to time, he asked them where Naro Penchung was in his climb. When they told him that he was not far from the summit, Milarepa pointed his finger in the direction of the drum, and it was immediately stopped. It could go neither up nor down. Then, Milarepa turned his head and, in an instant, he was on the mountain summit. By his own power, he made Naro Penchung climb to the summit. "You have lost the contest," he told him, "nevertheless, I will allow you to live on the small mountain you see there."

These wonders accomplished by Milarepa illustrate that all is possible after one has realized the empty nature of phenomena.

Question: Rinpoche has told us during an evening that it is possible to deal with emotions by simply looking at their essence, with the result that they will disappear by themselves. I see this possibility for anger and desire, because these emotions carry some energy that makes them present. However, I do not see how we can apply it to blindness or ignorance, which by definition keeps the mind in apathy and darkness. How is this possible?

Kalu Rinpoche: One must react to this apathy with diligence. This is possible by praying to the lama, the *yidam*, or the Three Jewels. In order to be cured with this method, all emotions require a certain will, necessary to react to the power of desire and anger, or the weight of torpor.

If one looks at the essence of emotions, if one does not allow oneself to be carried away by them, it is a source of great peace. Supposing you truly apply this method for one, two, or three years, this would be wonderful. There would no longer be any argument among you. I would receive a letter from Lama Tsewang Gyurme[29] telling me how Vancouver has become such a wonderful place!

Question: Shakyamuni Buddha was the fourth Buddha manifested in our kalpa. When can we expect the coming of Maitreya, who will be the fifth Buddha?

Kalu Rinpoche: Maitreya is now a bodhisattva on the tenth level. He has the capability of producing many emanations in order to work for the benefit of all beings. It is not impossible that some of these emanations are now present on Earth, but I cannot tell when Maitreya will effectively incarnate as the fifth Buddha.

Question: One hears a lot of talk about living initiation lineages and very powerful masters of achievement. If they are so powerful, why have they not solved the problems of the planet?

Kalu Rinpoche: It is necessary to understand that each individual has to experience the result of his or her own karma. If this were not true, the compassion of the Buddhas would have liberated all beings of the six classes long ago. Consciousness functions at an individual level and not at a collective level. Otherwise, it would suffice that one person feels a certain desire and the entire world would feel it at the same time. *Vancouver, B.C., Canada 1982*

---

[29]Lama in charge of a Buddhist center in Vancouver, Canada.

Scattered Flowers

HUMAN CONDITION

Our type of existence belongs to the class of superior beings, since we possess what one calls the "good human existence." It is good if it comprehends a certain liberty of body, speech and mind. We can choose to reside at a determined place or move, to speak or not speak, and so on. This freedom allows us to study and practice the Dharma and progress toward Awakening. However, this is far from a total freedom. Even if we wish for only fortunate circumstances, contrary to our will, we have to experience painful situations. Even if we do not want to become old but stay young forever, contrary to our will, months and years inescapably lead us to old age. Even if we do not want to become ill, contrary to our desire, illness will make us suffer.

From the viewpoint of its spiritual value, human existence is divided into three categories: superior, average, and inferior.

• A superior existence belongs to those people who are born in a country where spirituality is alive. They meet masters from whom they receive teachings; they feel attracted to the spiritual path and practice it. Given that it allows beings to progress toward Awakening, it is called the "precious" human existence.

• Average existence defines the category of people who are not especially concentrating on the practice of a spiritual path, performing positive acts, or accomplishing negative acts; they devote themselves only to temporal activities. This is true of a great number of people. It is an average existence in the sense that it produces neither a very good nor a very bad future life.

• Finally, inferior existence refers to those who, not knowing the Dharma, accomplish serious negative acts. It is inferior because it leads immediately after death to a rebirth in the hell realms, or rebirth as an animal, or in another type of existence marked by intense suffering.

Inferior and average human existences are numerous. They form 95 percent of the population of the planet. Only 5 percent of the population possesses the precious human existence. At best, it allows one to reach Awakening in one lifetime, or at least obtain a future, happy, divine, or human existence, with the potential to progress to ultimate Awakening. Now that we are endowed with this precious existence, it is necessary for us to give it full value by developing the three following qualities together:

- faith and confidence in the Dharma
- the spiritual intelligence that comes from a continuous study of the Dharma
- and a diligent and regular practice based on faith and intelligence

Perhaps you think that you do not have the time to practice the Dharma, that you will see to it later. But, do you know the hour of your death? When death approaches, if you find your life was not meaningful and has not reached any positive results, you will feel an immense regret. Imagine someone who obtained 200 pounds of gold. What wealth! But, if the person loses the gold before taking advantage of it, it is a huge loss. Dying without having made positive use of human existence is an even greater loss.

Taishung, March 24, 1986

THE TWO DHARMAS

Activities of the world can be divided in two categories: temporal dharma and spiritual Dharma.

Temporal dharma is designated as any activity accomplished to provide well-being in this life, such as working in the fields, an office, a factory, or elsewhere, in order to have food, shelter, clothing, and a comfortable life. Although it is useful for this life, it is useless for lives to come. During the night, we dream. It sometimes happens that we have beautiful dreams. When we wake up, the charm disappears; the dream world totally ceases to exist. It is the same when we die. All appearances of this world cease to exist. What we have done to make them pleasant is not useful for future lives.

On the other hand, the spiritual Dharma is useful in this life, and for lives to come. Why is it useful for this life? Our personality is composed of body, speech, and mind, the mind being the main element. At first, the spiritual Dharma gives peace and happiness, then freedom. Its effect on lives to come is even greater. An extremely deep spiritual practice allows us to obtain high levels of realization, by which it is possible, after death, to create many emanations of oneself, and send them to help all beings. If one's practice is not this profound, it is possible to be born in the Land of Bliss or in another Pure Land; at least, to once again obtain a good, divine, or human existence allowing oneself to make progress toward Awakening.

Depending on one's aspiration, it is possible to follow these two Dharmas separately or together. Milarepa chose the first option. Renouncing all temporal activity, he went into solitude to devote himself exclusively to the spiritual practice that allowed him to attain Awakening in one lifetime. As for Marpa, he married, had children, cultivated the fields, and was a trader. This example can only be followed by joining deep inner practice with an excellent comprehension of the Dharma. Because of the power of his meditation, his life did not prevent him from attaining liberation. A radically different manner of practice was the one used by King Indraboddhi during Buddha Shakyamuni's time. He governed a powerful and wealthy kingdom in the region of today's Kashmir and he enjoyed the company of 500 consorts during the day and 500 others at night.

Taishung, March 23, 1986

DO WE HAVE THE TIME?

All the beings of the six classes experience suffering; however, in each class certain aspects dominate. In the human world, there are four great sufferings:
- the suffering of birth
- the suffering of old age
- the suffering of sickness
- the suffering of death

There are two other sufferings specific to humankind. Human beings are always feeling that something is lacking, and they always are busy. "Lacking" means that human beings always have the sense that something is missing. Whether rich or poor, they unceasingly want something more, something that seems indispensable.

"Being busy" refers to the continual activity of human beings. They always are busy working, traveling, trading, discussing, eating, or doing a thousand other activities. They have no free time.

Some people are aware that the cycle of existences is, above all, suffering, and that it is necessary to liberate oneself from it. To liberate oneself implies study and the practice of a spiritual path, using body, speech, and mind; each appears to be different even though they are one in essence.

For example, the body can be put to use by taking the posture of meditation, making prostrations, offering *mandalas*, and so on. Unfortunately, we usually have no time to sit in meditation, no time to make prostrations, no time to offer *mandalas*, because we are too busy working, traveling, trading, and so on.

As for speech, it can be used to recite mantras or prayers. One can also keep silent and hold one's breath, or concentrate on the incoming and outgoing of the breath. But, again, we have no time to recite mantras or for remaining silent, because we are too busy talking without mindfulness.

As for the mind, picture an image. When the sky is clear during the day, it is a clear, infinite, empty space. Similarly, the true nature of the mind is infinite emptiness and clarity. Dwelling in this state is dwelling in peace and happiness. But, we have no time to taste this peace and happiness, because our mind is constantly busy, occupied by the passions of desire, hatred, opacity, pride, jealousy, greed, and their consequences. Even if we are not agitated by these passions, we are preoccupied with our business, our work, our family, our projects, and a lot of other things. There is no time to establish the mind in its true nature.

Generally, human beings simply do not make time to practice the Dharma, neither with body, speech, nor with the mind. Modern times have developed some techniques that make the situation worse; movies and television have swallowed what little available time was left.

We now have the human existence, and with it we have the opportunity to work for liberating ourselves from the cycle of existence and attaining Awakening. Moreover, we have met the Dharma and qualified masters. This spiritual color transforms our existence into a "precious human existence." It is necessary to take advantage of it. If you are in a situation where there is no time to effectively put your body to practice, you will gain something if, finding yourself in the presence of a sacred representation such as a statue or a spiritual master, you show respect, even if only by joining hands. Some mantras, like those of Akshobya (Tibetan, Mitrukpa) or Vajrasattva (Tibetan, Dorje Sempa), are perhaps too long for recitation. However, a mantra like the one of Avalokita (Tibetan, Chenrezig) has only six syllables (OM MANI PADME HUNG) and does not require a particular situation to recite it. One can recite it at the same time that one engages in any other activity, whether sitting, walking, being idle or at work, at night as well as during the day.

If you have no time to apply your mind in meditation, you nevertheless can make beneficial use of it by simply recalling, from time to time, the greatness of the Three Jewels and praying to them with sincerity for yourself and all beings to reach Awakening. Or, if you develop at least a little compassion for all beings who suffer, you will gain something. When you feel happy, think that it is an effect of the grace and compassion of the Three Jewels. When you feel miserable, think of the painful circumstances that you encounter as an expression of the compassion of the Three Jewels. Why? Because they allow you to experience now, in a relatively bearable way, the effect of a bad karmic potential that would have been expressed after your death in the form of circumstances incomparably more painful, as a birth in a hell world or in some other type of inferior existence.

If you are poor, do not be bothered by it. Think that it is the result of previous karma. Since you have not, in your past life, gathered the necessary karmic conditions to live in abundance in this life, you should be satisfied with what you have now. If, on the contrary, you are wealthy in this life, you should not be greedy but give as much as you can to the Three Jewels, to your spiritual masters, as well as those who are in need. At the moment of death, it will be necessary for you to leave all belongings behind. You will not be able to take any material object with you into the life to come. If you use your wealth to practice offering and giving, you accumulate a karmic potential that will actualize in future lives in the form of material ease. By acting like that, even if you cannot put time aside, at least be sure that your body, speech, and mind make some spiritual progress.

Hong Kong, March 20, 1986

THE EMOTIONS OF EACH PERSON

The total number of conflicting emotions is traditionally fixed at 84,000. All ordinary beings are afflicted, but there is some predominance according to people and countries. Tibetans have all the conflicting emotions, but for them the strongest is, without any doubt, anger. It was not rare that people, under its influence, fought until they killed each other.[30] Westerners have all conflicting emotions, but among them desire-attachment dominates; this is the source of multiple problems and suffering.

Chinese people have all the conflicting emotions, but jealousy and pride seem to be stronger in their case. It is important to know how to recognize the strongest conflicting emotion in oneself, because the first step taken should be an attempt to diminish its influence by practicing the Dharma.

Taipei, April 30, 1986

WORSE THAN WAR

Most people get married. For what reason? Because they believe this can make them happy. Nevertheless, if you do not maintain a harmonious relationship with your spouse and the members of your family, you work against the objective you have set for yourself by getting married. Nowadays, people fear another world war will happen. It is a frightening prospect, but perhaps these fears are exaggerated. It is true that such a war would produce immense suffering for two or three years. However, if you do not get along with your spouse, this suffering will last until death.

Hong Kong, March 20, 1986

---

[30] This characteristic was more particularly the mark of the people living in the province of Kham where Kalu Rinpoche was born.

In some countries, one can hardly find people suffering from real poverty. Instead, one will see people who suffer from being too wealthy. This seems to be a paradox.

The following story illustrates the problem. At the time of the Buddha, one of the monks of the community happened to possess a "magical jewel."[31] He led a simple existence and lived on alms. What need could he have of this jewel? It was better to give it to a poor person. But there were so many poor people! Who would he choose? Not knowing what to do, he went to see the Buddha and asked him for advice. "I possess a magical jewel and I do not need it for myself. I would like to give it to a poor person, but I am embarrassed and cannot decide to whom I should give it."

"Very well, give it to King Saja," answered the Buddha. "He is the poorest of all human beings."

However, this king was extremely wealthy. Without hesitating, the monk went to the palace, was introduced to the king and gave him the present. The king received the monk, and asked him the reason for his visit, if he had some request. The monk replied that such was not the case. He simply wanted to offer this jewel to a poor person, and the Buddha had designated the king as the poorest man in the kingdom. It is useless to describe the astonishment of the monarch. Covered with wealth and yet considered to be the poorest in the kingdom! This was a very strange pronouncement of the Buddha! Wanting to be sure, he went to the Buddha for an adequate explanation.

"A monk came to see you, asking you to indicate a poor person to whom he could give his magic jewel. Although

---

[31]The "magical jewel" (literally "the jewel that grants all wishes") was a kind of Aladdin's lamp in ancient India. To have it accomplish one's purpose, it was sufficient to express a wish.

there is no richer or more powerful man than I in this country, you told him to give the jewel to me. Why?"

"It is true, King Saja, you are the richest and most powerful man in the kingdom," replied the Buddha. "But your greed is so great that you are never satisfied with what you have. You live in constant fear that your possessions will be exhausted, and you constantly desire to amass new ones. Your mind is unceasingly tormented by the thirst for wealth, and this torment makes you the poorest of men. This is why I told the monk to give you the jewel."

Whatever our belongings, whether we possess very little or we live in abundance, it is our mental attitude that makes us rich or poor. If we have inner contentment, we will be happy; if not, we will be miserable despite all the wealth that we accumulate.

Taipei, April 15, 1986

VARIOUS TRADITIONS

The Buddha was born in India, 2913 years ago.[32] He became awakened in Bodhgaya and expounded the Dharma for the first time in Deer Park, near Benares. Buddhism is an ancient tradition that was first propagated in India, then China, Tibet, Mongolia, and many other countries in Asia. Christ's teachings are not as old, since we are now in the year 1987 of the Christian era. Other doctrines, for example the Muslim religion, appeared even later. The purpose of all these traditions is to help beings through varied approaches and methods. Since all have this function, all are basically good. How useful is all this diversity? When we are hungry, we can

---

[32]There are several dates concerning the birth of Shakyamuni Buddha. According to the scholars' calculations, he would have lived 536 to 480 B.C.E. which would place his birth 2523 years before the date of this teaching (1987). However, Kalu Rinpoche refers here to another system, to Kalachakra Tantra, that places this event 400 years earlier.

go to a restaurant. However, the restaurant does not display just one dish, because this would not suit everyone's taste. On the contrary, it offers a varied menu. Similarly, the aspirations of people in the spiritual domain are diversified and require teachings that are also diversified.

Madrid, Autumn 1987

BUDDHISM AND THE WEST

One can find three reasons for the expansion of Buddhism in the West.

- Some people, having heard about Tibet and Tibetans, conceived a favorable opinion and went to India, where they were able to meet Tibetan masters. Observing how the teachings benefitted them, they invited many lamas and tulkus to come to the West.

- The values shared by Christianity and Buddhism have prepared favorable ground: devotion (for God or the Three Jewels), the love and the compassion for beings, the respect for ethics, and so on.

- For the most part, Westerners have been studying a lot, and have developed their intelligence. They can understand the deep aspects of Buddhism more easily.

Madrid, Autumn 1987

RECEIVING THE TEACHING

To receive the Dharma, we need to be a "good vessel." To be so, it is necessary to avoid three defects.

If we attend a teaching by merely hearing it rather than listening to it, we resemble an upside down container. We can pour as much water as we want over it; nothing will penetrate it. Therefore, we should be very attentive to the teachings given to us.

However, it is not sufficient to listen correctly, it is also necessary to remember what is being said; lacking that, we are like a container full of holes. It receives water, but releases it immediately.

Finally, it is also necessary that the container be pure, in other words that our conflicting emotions do not mix with the received teaching. If, for example, desire, anger, or torpor disturbs our mind at the moment we receive the Dharma, it is said that it is like poison mixed with good food. At the moment, the poisoned food may appear delicious to us, but sooner or later, it will harm us. The power of conflicting emotions, in the same manner, may overcome the beneficial characteristics of the Dharma.

During a teaching, the right attitude is to be attentive, to retain what is explained and receive it with confidence and joy, reminding ourselves that it presents ways to reach Awakening and benefit beings.

The context of Vajrayana requires a special attitude. Vajrayana implies transformation of the impure into the pure. A teaching of this vehicle should be received thinking that we are not in an ordinary place, but in a pure land such as the Field of Bliss, taking into account that the lama who gives it is not an ordinary being, but a *yidam*, a Buddha, or a bodhisattva. We should look at the assembled people as a meeting of gods and goddesses. We should also think that the word of the master is union of sound and emptiness, endowed with the 60 qualities of the word of a Buddha.

Kagyu Ling, May 1980

PROGRESS OF A NONGIFTED MONK

It is not easy to reach Buddhahood. Since time without beginning, under the influence of ignorance and latent conditioning, we have reinforced the veils of conflicting emotions and karma. Time and energy are needed to undo these obstructions. The rapidity of our progression depends on our capabilities; depending on whether they are superior, average, or inferior, we progress very rapidly, rapidly, or slowly.

This does not mean that inferior capabilities are an obstacle beyond remedy. It is always possible to purify oneself and accumulate merit. One cites the case, at the time of the Buddha, of a monk, Lha Drente, whose intellectual abilities were so limited that he could not even assimilate the first letters of the alphabet. His faith, however, was immense.

Observing his incapacity, other monks asked the Buddha if there was a remedy. The Buddha replied that it was sufficient for Lha Drente to avoid all negative acts and devote himself to simple positive acts. He commanded that the task of cleaning the temple be given to this monk. During many years, Lha Drente devoted himself to sweeping the temple and scrubbing the offering bowls on the altars.

Little by little, this very simple task dissipated the veils of his mind so that his intelligence awakened. He succeeded in understanding the teachings the Buddha delivered on the Four Noble Truths and the twelve interdependent links and reached the state of an *arhat*. He is one of the sixteen Elders (Sanskrit, *Staviras*), often represented on *tangkas*.

Kagyu Ling, May 1980

THE MAN WITH A DIAMOND EAR

Purification and accumulation of merit have infallible results.

A long time ago, a merchant who hardly had any spiritual practice walked near a stupa, and felt not only a surge of faith, but an unusual joy. On the spot, he took the earring that he wore and deposited it as an offering on the monument.

By this offering, he engendered such great merit that he was reborn in the superior worlds, as human or a god during many lives.

At the time of the Buddha, a boy was born into a noble family. He had the distinction of having a diamond naturally set in his ear. Therefore, he earned the nickname of "the man whose ear costs a million." He was gifted, handsome, intelligent, and very articulate. He had assimilated all the arts of his time. When he became an adult, he met the Buddha, received ordination from him, and attained the state of an *arhat*.

Curious about this course of events, some monks asked the Buddha to explain. Why did this man have this diamond in his ear? Why did he give up wealth in this world? and why this sudden attainment of *arhatship*? The Buddha, who knew the karma of all beings, told them the story of the offering of the earring on the stupa, and explained that the diamond resulted from the nature of this offering. Faith in the Buddha and realization of *arhatship* were the result of the destination of the offering, which was to the stupa, a symbol of the Awakened mind.

Kagyu Ling, May 1980

SAVING MERIT

The accumulation of merit is useful not only for this life, but also for future lives. As long as the fruit is not harvested, benefit is never lost.

Some circumstances risk neutralizing positive accomplished acts. For example, let us suppose you had accomplished an important offering, and that you felt some vanity, or regret at having spent too much. This vanity or regret damages the positive value of generosity. More serious is anger, since it is said that a single outbreak of anger can reduce to nothing 100 *kalpas* of positive acts.

However, the Buddha has taught a way that allows us to save the merit of acts. It is to dedicate them. Let us compare a positive act to a drop of water. Left in the sun, it risks sudden evaporation. Deposited in the sea, it dissolves in water, and will not evaporate unless the whole sea dries up. In the same manner, once dedication is made, the benefit of positive acts no longer disappears, even if conflicting emotions arise in our mind. On the contrary, because of dedication, merit never decreases; it is just like the interest on money placed in a bank that does not stop being added to the capital.

Dedication can be done in two ways: with an object or without an object.[33] As long as one has not achieved ultimate nature of the mind, this second type of dedication, which is the greatest, is not truly accessible. Nevertheless, to approach it, we can think that we dedicate merit as did the bodhisattvas of the past. This is why, in one of the traditional texts, it is said, referring to two great bodhisattvas:

According to the knowledge of suchness[34] of the courageous Manjushri,
And also that of Samantabhadra,
Following them,
I perfectly dedicate all these virtuous acts.

Kagyu Ling, May 1980

TRUE HAPPINESS

Because of positive karma resulting from their past lives, some people now enjoy great wealth. Some possess millions of dollars. However, this wealth does not grant happiness. True happiness, happiness of the mind, is difficult to obtain.

In the contemporary world, people are animated by feverish agitation. Many cannot stay quiet; they go from one place to another, visiting one country after another. This continual search for the new is a sign of lacking happiness.

---

[33]The dedication consists, for example, of the wish that the merit stemming from such and such positive act helps us to reach Awakening for the benefit of all beings. It is said to be "with object" when it is accomplished with a duality of subject-object; it is said to be "without object" when duality no longer is implied between a "me" and "another."

[34]The "suchness" refers to the absolute reality of all phenomena, beyond concepts and notions of me and other.

The mind, with its variety of distractions that monopolize it, wants to forget its feelings of frustration.

Practiced correctly, meditation allows us to pacify our mind, to make it stable and, by this way, to find inner well-being and an authentic happiness.

Our mind becomes tired of all the thoughts and conflicting emotions within it. Our body is equally tired due to following orders imposed by our agitated mind. Practicing meditation will bring more rest to our mind and body than a walk in a park full of flowers.

Kagyu Ling, May 1980

A HEALTHY REFLECTION

Milarepa was born in a well-to-do family. Unfortunately, when his father died, his uncle and aunt defrauded him of all his property. To seek revenge, his mother requested that he learn black magic and use it against them.

Obeying his mother, Milarepa left to study under a master of black magic and, being assiduous, he rapidly obtained some powers. He used them to destroy a house and provoke a hailstorm, which killed several people and a great number of animals and insects. He had committed several seriously harmful acts.

A short time later, he was filled with remorse and fear. He envisioned impermanence and death, and thought that he would be unable to escape the torments of hell. This prospect scared him so that he could no longer eat or sleep.

One of the main benefactors of the black magician passed away. Being very affected, the magician became conscious of the impermanence of all beings. Sharing with Milarepa, he told him, "Death inevitably waits for us; we have devoted our life to evil. Now we should repent and practice the Dharma while there is still time left. Choose! You can go in search of a lama who will teach you the right way, or I will practice the Dharma myself and you will be my assistant."

Milarepa chose the first alternative. The magician was happy. "You are young," he told his pupil "and you will be able to practice well. Myself, I am an old man and I no longer have much strength. Therefore it is a good decision." Milarepa left in quest of a master and met Marpa. After having received instructions, he practiced with extraordinary diligence, not relaxing day or night, abandoning all the benefits of this world. Reflecting on the precious human existence, impermanence, the law of karma, and on the suffering inherent in samsara, he drew upon a source of immense energy that allowed him to reach Awakening in a single lifetime.

Without filling ourselves with these four ideas just mentioned, it is difficult to turn toward the Dharma, or even if we follow the path, our practice would be like a sand castle, rapidly washed away by the waves. These four ideas in themselves do not lead to liberation, but they provide the energy that allows us to reach it.

Kagyu Ling, May 1980

HAVING NO WRONG VIEW ON EMPTINESS

We believe that phenomena are real, and this belief causes so much suffering. However, it is necessary to avoid the opposite extreme of thinking that everything is empty, in such a way that nothing exists at all. In this case, one will deduce that, the Three Jewels being empty, it is not useful to pray to them, and, the law of karma being empty, it is useless to respect it, and so on.

We should understand that the Buddha has taught emptiness with a precise purpose: neutralizing all concepts that one can attach to absolute truth. This prevents us from considering it as one or many nonexistent or existent objects, one or many, or an object defined by any characteristic, whatsoever. Thinking that emptiness is real is an error even greater than completely closing the doors to liberation. Nagarjuna said that the people who believe in the reality of the world are, in some ways, similar to animals, but that those who accept emptiness as real are even more stupid. It is also said that belief in the reality of phenomena is an error as large as Mount Meru, but that to become attached to emptiness is an even greater mistake.

As long as we have not attained liberation, the illusory appearances of relative truth remain real for us, and we have to consider this fact. As long as we are in a prison, we cannot act as if we were free.

Kagyu Ling, May 1980

EMPTINESS AND KARMA

Some people, believing that they understand the Dharma, imagine that it is sufficient to meditate on emptiness without being preoccupied with karma, since karma is ultimately empty. These people should try to spend a complete day without eating, drinking, or putting on clothes. If they feel neither hunger, nor thirst, nor cold, this will be the sign that everything is empty. Otherwise, it is necessary to conclude that everything is not entirely empty and the law of karma has some importance.

Kagyu Ling, May 1980

FLATTENING CREASES

People who know the Dharma for a very short time sometimes think that it allows them to reach Awakening in a few weeks or months. After a short time devoted to practice, they notice a lot has to be done. Many conflicting emotions still are affecting their mind, perhaps even more than before. They conclude that the Dharma is not efficient as they had thought after all, and they leave.

Let us recall that the unsettling of our mind was imprinted in our mind since time without beginning, engendering restrictive tendencies. It is like a sheet of paper that has remained rolled up for a long time; it takes considerable time to get it flat again. *Kagyu Ling, May 1980*

POWER OF FAITH

It has been taught by the Buddha that when a person sincerely prays to him, he is truly in front of this person. It is also said that where there is faith in the Three Jewels, the Three Jewels are manifested, just as the moon is reflected on the surface of water.

It has been said that a woman who possessed all the characteristics of a *dakini* had married a particularly obtuse, but fundamentally good man, animated by great faith. Wishing to help her husband, the woman advised him to turn toward Manjushri, the bodhisattva of knowledge, and also requested him to spend the night praying in front of a huge statue of the deity enshrined in the neighboring temple. "At dawn, you will close your eyes and open your hand; Manjushri will give you something that you will eat with complete trust; this will be his blessing."

The husband placed himself in front of the statue and spent the night fervently addressing prayers to Manjushri in order to become more intelligent. When the sun rose, he put forth his open hand toward the deity. His wife, hidden behind the statue, put a fruit in his hand and he ate it with immense devotion. Immediately, his intelligence lit up to such an extent that he later became a famous scholar.

When we pray to the Three Jewels and Three Roots with a sincere heart, they are really present.

Kagyu Ling, May 1980

NEITHER BLIND, NOR ARMLESS

It is said that practicing without studying is like a wandering blind person, and studying without practicing is like an armless person wanting to climb a cliff.

The field of Buddhist knowledge is extremely vast. Exploring it in its entirety, if one is capable, is very beneficial. Nevertheless, it is sufficient to understand the direct

instructions on the foundations of practice and
meditation—the instructions given to us by the lama.
Kagyu Ling, May 1980

ESSENCE OF THE TEACHING

It is said that the teachings given by the Buddha are as vast
as space and as deep as the ocean. Studying all their facets
would take an extremely long time. However, the most
important, essentials brought together are the direct
instructions given to us by our lama. We should listen to
them, reflect upon them and put them into practice. To follow
these instructions will soon appear beneficial.
New Delhi, February 1985

HUMAN OR ANIMAL?

At the present time, because of previous good karma, a great
development of intelligence is happening. In the field of
science and technology, many inventions and discoveries are
being made. Without the knowledge of mind, without
knowledge of what we truly are, there can be no difference
between us and animals.
Vajradharaling, 1984

TAKING THE PLANE

Without understanding the nature of mind, meditation is very
difficult; it is like driving a car on a bad road. However, from
the moment you know the nature of mind, meditation
becomes easy, as if you were flying in an airplane.
New Delhi, February 1985

POTENTIAL OF AWAKENING

The nature of the mind, which is emptiness, clarity, and
intelligence without obstruction, is shared by all the beings of
the six worlds. It is called the "potential for Awakening"

(Sanskrit, *tathagatagarbha*). Given that we possess all this potential, if we accomplish what is necessary, we can attain true Awakening. Suppose that a conch, covered with mud, has become black. As it is white by nature, if you clean it, it will recover its whiteness. On the contrary, rub a piece of coal as long as you want, it will never become white. Similarly, if we did not possess the potential for Awakening, nothing would allow us to ever reach Awakening.

New Delhi, February 1985

THE TRUE SCIENTIST

Not knowing our own mind is like a blind person who does not know how to find the way and who feels around for all he or she wants to do. This is not only valid for the Dharma, but also for our ordinary activity.

Nowadays, there are extremely learned people capable of presenting elaborate descriptions of the universe and matter, discovering the most subtle laws in physics and chemistry. But when one asks a question about the nature of the mind, nobody answers.

The science of the mind, the description of its nature, in fact, was expounded by the Buddha a long time ago. Even if we no longer can meet with him as a person, his teaching continues to be transmitted and placed at our disposal as a science we can study. You will approach it more easily because the years that you spent in school or at the university have developed your intellectual capabilities. When you truly understand what the mind is, you will be a true scientist.

The mind is not far away; we always have it with us. Therefore, studying it does not require us to go somewhere or to possess any special equipment. A small piece of property, like Montchardon, has a great number of places, trees, plants, objects, and so on. If we were to look for the mind here, it would require some length of time. But the mind is within us;

what difficulty would we have in finding it? It is always there. Nothing is closer. Nothing should be easier than finding it.

Many people believe themselves to be learned and intelligent. However, as long as the mind has not been found, one is neither truly learned nor truly intelligent.

Karma Migyur Ling, August 1987

SIGNS OF EMPTINESS

At the end of the *bardo*, your karma pushed you into a human birth. When your mind joined the physical supports of your father and mother, nobody saw it enter. As it is not a substance, it cannot be seen. At the moment of death, your mind will leave your body, and even if a hundred people are surrounding you, no one will see it escaping. These are signs of the emptiness of mind.

New Delhi, February 1985

THE SHADOW OF KARMA

It is said that one cannot see the shadow of a bird gliding very high in the sky; however, that shadow becomes increasingly visible as the bird approaches the ground. In a same manner, we cannot see our karmic potential; but it becomes obvious when it actualizes itself.

New Delhi, February 1985

THE LESSON OF DEATH

One can see in Burma an immense statue representing the Buddha pointing a finger at a mother carrying the body of her dead child. This statue refers to an episode in the life of the Buddha.

A woman named Krisha Gotami had lost her child, and her sorrow was extreme. She went to see the Buddha requesting, that he resuscitate her child. The Buddha replied that he would do it on the condition that she bring him a handful of mustard seeds from a family that death had never touched. Krisha Gotami went from house to house, but everywhere she received a disappointing answer: "I lost my husband this year," "My child died three years ago," "My mother died in this bedroom," and so on. She went back to the Buddha to tell him, "Alas! Death had spared no family, it is the share of all human beings."

The Buddha, pointing to the child with his hand, told her, "Yes, that is it; you have understood. Death is a universal law. It makes no exception, not even for your child."

Many events can serve as a lesson.

New Delhi, February 1985

Human Existence

We now possess the ideal support of existence for practice of the Dharma, the precious human existence. Far from being the fruit of chance, the human condition is foremost of the superior worlds in the system of the six classes of beings, and results from the conjunction of several elements from past lives:
- a vast accumulation of merit
- less negative activity than positive activity
- connection with the Buddha, the Dharma, or Sangha

Without meeting these factors, the precious human existence cannot be obtained.

RARE AS STARS DURING THE DAY

The number of beings is incalculable because they are infinite in number. However, texts use comparisons to give an idea of the relative quantity of beings in every possible existence:
- beings who populate the eighteen types of hell are said to be as numerous as atoms composing the planet Earth
- hungry ghosts are as numerous as grains of sand forming the bottom of an ocean or the bed of a long river
- animals are as numerous as snowflakes falling during a storm in winter

These comparisons show that beings from the three inferior worlds are innumerable.

As for those of the three superior worlds together—human, demi-gods, and gods—their quantity equals that of the stars of the night sky. This number seems very large, but compared to that of inferior worlds, it remains small. Without a doubt, the quantity of the human beings residing on our planet alone appears important. But this is only relative. Without mentioning hell beings and hungry ghosts we cannot see, if we consider the realm of animals, we observe that they are infinitely more numerous than we are.

THREE CATEGORIES OF HUMAN BEINGS

In general, merit and karma are the causes of obtaining human existence, but the quality of karma varies according to people. Three categories are envisioned:

- Inferior human existence is the existence of those having no knowledge of a spiritual way, or who have no interest in it and continually accomplish serious negative acts. Their existence is called "inferior," not in itself, but in the prospect of the karmic result that it entails. After death, it leads to a birth in inferior worlds, and there one experiences great suffering.

- Mediocre human existence refers to those who accomplish neither great negative acts nor great positive acts and devote all their efforts to ordinary activities of this world. It includes the vast majority of human beings. This existence is mediocre from the point of view of karma. It will entail a type of mediocre rebirth, neither low nor high, not comprising the possibility of being reborn in divine kingdoms, or of even reaching Buddhahood.

- Finally, there are those who reject negative acts, and on the contrary, find joy in accomplishing positive acts. They possess a superior human existence. In their future lives, they will be born in the best conditions in the world of humans, or in divine realms. Better yet, those who come in contact with the Dharma, follow the teaching of masters, and receive instructions of the Hinayana, Mahayana, or Vajrayana, form the "superior among the superior existences" called the "precious" human existence.

MORE PRECIOUS THAN A DIAMOND

If you use the example of the country where you live, you will see easily that most of its residents can be classified in the category of an inferior or a mediocre existence. Very few are those who avoid negative acts and cherish positive conduct. Among them, still more rare, are those who have made contact with the Dharma and follow the teaching of the masters. They are compared to stars shining in a daylight sky.

This distribution of human beings was taught by the Buddha and continues to be taught by the lamas. You can also observe this by yourself. Among the millions of people who reside in your country, how many are interested in a spiritual path, how many practice it, and how many follow a master?

Diamond and gold are substances whose rarity determines their price. In the case of a human existence, it is not only its rarity that confers value, but that the human existence abounds in wealth. You know the holy Dharma, you have met lamas, you have received teachings and instructions, and you possess all conditions favorable to practice. Because of this, you can liberate yourself from the ocean of samsaric suffering and reach the definitive and authentic happiness of Awakening. You now have this extraordinary human existence so difficult to obtain—you should become deeply conscious of it.

Having this consciousness should not lead us to pride, but rather to a feeling of responsibility. We should always make the best use of the situation and use it to attain Buddhahood. To do so, we should put our body, speech, and mind in its service. If we waste these circumstances that are extraordinary and difficult to obtain, and if we let them pass without using them, how can we hope to find them again?

LIMITS OF THE TEMPORAL DOMAIN

In the course of our life, we continue to follow temporal or spiritual goals. The precious human existence offers the potential to reach both. We often think that the Dharma is a good thing, but it is equally important to concern ourselves with this present life. In a certain sense, it is true that this world is not to be neglected. It is necessary for us to eat correctly, to dress decently, to live in good conditions, and so on. It is normal to take care of these things. However, the importance of all that we can accomplish in the temporal domain is made relative by our certain death, which makes it amount to nothing.

The efforts we use to reach our objectives in this life can take two turns. Either, we will not have sufficient karma for our efforts to succeed; or, we will have the necessary karma and, according to what we wish, we will obtain wealth, reputation, and so on. However, even then, our success will not be eternal. It is necessarily limited by death, leaving behind nothing more than a dream. We may dream of living in a magnificent region, residing in a beautiful house, having all that we wish, and living as happily as a god. When we wake up, everything disappears, nothing remains. Our wealth and well-being in this world are similar to this dream. In fact, death makes us exit into the *bardo*. Temporal belongings are far from possessing all the value we attribute to them.

APPRECIATING OUR CAPABILITIES

In the Buddhist tradition in general, and particularly in the framework of the four great Tibetan lineages, when approaching the practice of Dharma, one always begins by reflecting on this precious human existence in order to become conscious of its value. Through numerical relations, metaphors, and the study of causes, the disciple is brought to understand how difficult and rare it is to obtain. One understands how essential it is, now that human existence has been obtained, to make this existence meaningful by exclusively devoting oneself to spiritual practice with the goal of attaining Awakening.

We are able to better understand the specificity of human existence by comparing it to other types of existence. Let us take the case of animals, simply those closest to us: horses, cats, dogs, cows, and so on. Whatever their intelligence, you could try to explain to them the benefits of positive acts or the disadvantage of negative acts, yet they will understand nothing. You cannot teach them to pray, to meditate, or to develop love and compassion. From a spiritual point of view, their condition is disadvantageous; they have no possibility of making progress toward Awakening. We can, however, understand, explain, pray, and meditate.

HARMFUL DESIRE-ATTACHMENT

The mind of all beings in samsara is afflicted by the six basic conflicting emotions, not in an equal manner, but with dominant traits prevailing.

Humans belong to the realm called the "sphere of desire" with the result that they are strongly marked by desire and attachment. By desire-attachment one does not refer exclusively to sexual desire but to all variants that this emotion can take in relationship to people, objects, or situations.

We are fortunate to have obtained a precious human existence and be aware of it. That does not prevent the force of conflicting emotions to manifest itself in our spirit. Because of the teachings given by the Buddha, we have a large array of methods for dealing with conflicting emotions, different techniques of rejection, transformation, or recognition of their essence so that we should not become their slave.

Conflicting emotions are the source of all negative acts, and consequently, all suffering. This is why it is important to solve the problems they create. Their suppression automatically necessitates the elimination of negative acts and suffering. It is absolutely mandatory to know how to deal with them.

Of all the conflicting emotions, desire-attachment appears, affectively, to be the least harmful in and of itself. Unfortunately, it is followed by anger, jealousy, pride, possessiveness, a complete retinue revealing itself to be very harmful. The final result is much suffering and misfortune.

Doing nothing to eliminate emotions, but letting oneself be carried away by them, allows them to flow as a river. One can be sure water will not cease to flow. In the same way, emotions will continually be followed by new emotions and, as inevitably, by new negative acts and suffering. Perhaps we cannot attack emotions head-on and reject them, but the Buddha taught other approaches for transforming them or learning to recognize their essence, neutralizing them in an efficient manner, and liberating ourselves from them.

RAZING THE MOUNTAIN OF NEGATIVE ACTS

Personality is formed by three components, body, speech, and mind, through which we can be led to commit negative acts.
- with the body: killing, stealing, or engaging in incorrect sexual conduct
   - through speech: lying, using harmful words, slander, and idle chatter
   - with the mind: covetousness, ill-wish, and erroneous views

Our entire person is implicated in negativity. This process has been so since time without beginning. During numberless different existences, our body, speech, and mind, have served to produce negative karma. Its quantity could be compared to an ocean without limit or to the axial mountain of the universe. Now, we should rid ourselves of negativity. Good human existence offers us some possibilities.

Although human life is brief, if used wisely, it allows for the elimination of the immense potential of negative acts within us. Accumulated by body, speech, and mind, negative potential can also be neutralized by the same agents.

- the body, concentrating on prostrations and giving
- speech, the recitation of prayers, rituals and mantras such as that of Vajrasattva (Tibetan, Dorje Sempa) or Avalokita (Tibetan, Chenrezig)
- the mind: the different types of meditation, such as mental calming, superior vision, phases of creation and completion of the Vajrayana, and development of love and compassion

The totality of these exercises will certainly help reduce to nothingness the mountain of negative karma.

IMPORTANCE OF PHYSICAL AND ORAL EXERCISES

It is true that the mind is more important than body and speech because it governs them. It is the reason a person who has received the instructions on mahamudra, or maha-ati, and is capable of genuine meditation, can maintain an internal state no longer affected by body activity (motion, sitting, sleeping, eating, or doing nothing, and so on) or speech. This person knows the real nature of the mind and can remain there without distraction. The use of body and speech no longer concerns him or her. This constant recognition of the nature of the mind is extremely difficult.

Those who are incapable of doing this and who think they can dispense with oral and physical exercises and still progress are greatly mistaken. These exercises are important supports for realization. For example, it is obvious that physical posture greatly enhances meditation.

THE YOGI AND THE MONKEY

This is the story of a yogi who used to meditate in a forest inhabited by a large tribe of monkeys. The yogi constantly maintained a perfect posture. The chief of the monkeys, who without a doubt possessed some positive karmic tendencies, found it very amusing to imitate the yogi. The monkey was so successful that his mind gradually became more peaceful, and he successfully entered a state of meditation. The members of his tribe did the same thing as their chief, as was their habit. The result was that all the monkeys achieved great inner peace. This story underlines the impact of the use of the body solely, without any other mental preparation.

Speech can play a role just as important, notably in the use of mantras. It is said that meditation is similar to fire, and recitation of mantras similar to the wind that makes it burn.

MEDITATION OF THE CROCODILES

Everybody considers meditation important, deep, and useful. Still, it is necessary to understand what it is. Sometimes, one can think that it is simply remaining still, in a sort of apathy. This will result only in strengthening the natural tendencies of torpor and ignorance. Sakyapandita said that the person who has not received the instructions of an authentic master, but who is happy to be rocked by his or her own torpor, does nothing else than prepare for rebirth in the animal world. He also said that numerous are those believing they practice mahamudra, but in fact, weave the bonds of a future rebirth in the animal world. We have a good idea of what Sakyapandita is saying by visiting a zoo. There, we will see crocodiles lying in the sun. Nothing can draw them out of their sleepiness. Neither screams nor thrown objects will move them. Hippopotami move only to yawn enormously, and there are many other animals whose mental characteristics are strongly marked by sleepiness and lack of alertness.

Whether one practices mental calming, superior vision, or mahamudra, one should do it with the perfect knowledge of what they are. At the same time, it is necessary to support meditation with devotion to the master, and compassion for all beings. All this is the function of the mind. If we add the work of speech to it, by frequent recitation of the mantra of Avalokita (Chenrezig) or other mantras, we will receive considerable help.

When one does not know how to meditate, and is happy to sit doing nothing allowing the mind to remain in a dull state, relatively devoid of thoughts, one will feel, it is true, a feeling of well-being linked to apathy. In Tibet, one can see marmots. During five or six months of the year, they hibernate underground without eating or drinking anything. They dwell in a torpor pleasing themselves, without thinking of anything, neither eating, urinating, or any kind of thinking whatsoever. When the six months of hibernation end, they climb out of their hole in good health and resume ordinary activity. They have passed six months in a cozy comfort, but no one can tell what they have accomplished on a spiritual level.

NOT SPOILING OUR GOOD LUCK

Now that we possess this precious human existence, let us apply body, speech, and mind to the Dharma and try to understand it fully. Even if we lack time, let us do it in short sessions as often as possible. Otherwise, we risk completely wasting the extraordinary opportunity that this life offers us. Let us recall that life is brief, similar to the flash of lightning that tears apart the night sky, and that we have no idea when it will end. If we have accomplished nothing spiritually, we will then leave empty-handed, without having gathered any of the jewels within our reach.

It is indispensable to continually reflect on impermanence, death, and the suffering inherent in samsara. When you hear the lama talking about these themes, it is possible you are not willing to listen, perhaps you even feel annoyed. It is nevertheless essential to understand them well. In Western languages, there are translations of various texts where they are approached in detail, and you can refer to them: the Torch of Certainty, the Jewel Ornament of Liberation or even small books that I have written.

Permeating ourselves with the ideas of impermanence and the unsatisfactory nature of samsara allows us to develop diligence for practice, diverts us from worldly pursuit, and urges us toward attaining Buddhahood.

WHIP COACHMAN!

Those who have been to India have seen there a lot of horse-drawn carriages. You have noticed how the coachman urges the horse forward by touching him with a stick. The more he hits the horse, the quicker the horse runs. In the same way, we need the stick of reflection on impermanence and suffering to make progress. Perhaps, up to now, you have not sufficiently used this stick and lack energy to cover the path of the Dharma.

When we read the life of Milarepa, we admire the force and extreme energy that he put into his practice. Neither death, sickness, cold weather, nor hunger, were able to stop him. This is because he had perfectly permeated himself with the notions of the precious human existence, impermanence, karma, and suffering.

THE OLD LADY IN HAWAII

When I went to Hawaii in 1978, an elderly lady came to see me and told me the following story.

"When you taught on the West coast, I found it very interesting. But, why did you speak so much about hell and hungry ghosts? It was very unpleasant to listen to this! Please, for the teachings that you will be giving in Hawaii, do not repeat such horrors!" I then had to give a seminar on meditation lasting several days, and it appeared impossible for me to approach the subject without mentioning the different worlds. When I started to talk about the inferior worlds, I saw the poor lady leaving the room.

Samye Ling, March 1983

Young Kalu Rinpoche (July 1992)
His father, Lama Gyaltsen Ratak
His mother, Kalzang Drolkar

Buddhist Perspectives

The teaching presented here approaches, in a few pages, a great number of themes that were dear to Kalu Rinpoche. Historical aspects of the transmission, nature of mind, the four veils, karma, consciousnesses, the foundations of the path, the different worlds, the value of the human existence, refuge, and the functioning of illusion are surveyed here. This overall view is only a brief introduction. These themes are seen again and developed further in the two other volumes of our trilogy: Profound Buddhism and Secret Buddhism.

Being omniscient and having pure love, the Buddha possesses the power to help all beings. This power is limited by our capacities; if we do not have the necessary inner opening, gained from our merit and karma, we have no possibility of meeting and understanding his teachings.

FROM INDIA TO TIBET

In our cosmic era, three Buddhas manifested before Shakyamuni Buddha. The latter lived in India more than 2500 years ago; it is said that 996 other Buddhas will follow him.

Shakyamuni Buddha, after accomplishing twelve great acts, began his vast activity for the benefit of all beings. In particular, he gave a variety of teachings that engendered many sages in India. It is said that they are as numerous as stars in the sky.

In Tibet, Buddhism was introduced because of the aspiration and activity of kings, who were manifestations of bodhisattvas. They invited Indian masters to the country and trained Tibetan translators. The translators had learned

Sanskrit and, with numerous difficulties, went to India and studied the Dharma in order to bring it to Tibet. One of the most famous translators, Marpa, during his travels to the country of origin of Buddhism, received teachings from Naropa and many other masters. Having obtained realization, he himself had many disciples in Tibet, notably Milarepa, who was acclaimed as the sun of the Dharma rising on Tibet. Marpa is at the origin of the Kagyupa lineage. Lamas receiving teachings in India from other masters have introduced different transmission lineages to Tibet. Today, four lineages remain preeminent: Nyingmapa, Kagyupa, Sakyapa, and Gelukpa. They all carry the teachings of the Buddha.

Just as Buddhism formerly passed from India to Tibet, it is now being transmitted from Tibet to the West by numerous lamas who sought refuge in India because of the Chinese invasion.

BASIS ON THE DHARMA

When one speaks of the Dharma of the Buddha, what is it fundamentally? The Dharma provides us with spiritual benefits. First of all, one must have an attitude of love and compassion, directed toward benefitting others. On this basis, it is important to understand the mind, the driving force of mental activity. How is it? What is it? By meditating, one begins to have an idea of its nature, and gains some control of the mind. This allows us to turn away from samsara and enter the path of liberation.

INNER BUDDHA PATH

Among numerous spiritual traditions in the world, we now study Buddhism. It is called, "Inner Way of the Buddha" in Tibetan. This expression refers to the founder of the tradition, and it also means that it concerns the mind which is the inner part of a person, similar to the inhabitant of a house.

It has been told by the Buddha:
All beings are Buddhas,
But their mind is obscured by adventitious impurities.
Once impurities are dissipated, beings are truly Buddhas.

Indeed, all beings possess Buddha nature, or the potential for Awakening. This Buddha-mind contains infinite qualities. They are all ours at this very moment but as our mind is covered with veils, they remain latent. Once these veils are dissipated, these qualities appear completely.

THE FOUR VEILS

There are four veils. Since time without beginning, the mind does not recognize itself; it does not recognize its real nature and does not see itself. This is the veil of ignorance.

From this fundamental ignorance a deep dysfunctioning arises. The total purity of an Awakened mind expresses itself with three modes called the three Bodies of the Buddha, the Absolute Body (Sanskrit, *dharmakaya*), the Body of Perfect Experience (Sanskrit, *sambhogakaya*), and the Body of Emanation (Sanskrit, *nirmanakaya*). Under the grasping of ignorance, however, the mind, not recognizing its own emptiness that corresponds to the Absolute Body, conceives an illusory "me" with which it identifies itself.

The mind is not only empty, it is also clarity, which means that it is able to produce all kinds of thoughts. All phenomena appear in the mind. Taking this clarity as distinct in itself, the mind conceives "another," and a polarity is formed, "me" and "another" creating a basis for the veil of latent conditionings.

A third aspect of the mind is knowledge, which is also called "non-obstruction" and it is linked both to emptiness and clarity. When the mind, basing itself on the duality "me/other," does not recognize this power of knowing itself, it becomes attached to pleasant objects, pushes away unpleasant objects, and remains in blind ignorance of the true nature of phenomena. Instead of unobstructed knowing, the three basic conflicting emotions—attraction, aversion, and ignorance—arise. They divide themselves into numerous ramifications, finally forming a network of 84,000 emotions constituting the third veil, that of conflicting emotions.

Under the influence of conflicting emotions, we accomplish with body, speech, and mind, many acts that are mostly negative. They lead to birth into the six worlds where happiness or suffering are felt, depending on each person's previous acts. It is this link which causes samsara to happen. It forms the fourth veil, the veil of karma.

These are the four great veils that cover the mind: the veil of ignorance, the veil of latent conditioning, the veil of conflicting emotions, and the veil of karma. Those whose mind is covered by these four veils are called ordinary beings.

INDIVIDUALIZED CONSCIOUSNESS

As a prisoner of these four veils, the mind produces many mental manifestations, which are ordinary thoughts. The mind then functions according to a mode called "individualized consciousness." This individualized consciousness has eight facets.

- First of all, the basis for functioning is the "potential of individualized consciousness." From it, the sense consciousnesses arise which perceive the world through the corresponding body organs:
    - visual consciousness
    - auditory consciousness
    - olfactory consciousness
    - gustatory consciousness
    - tactile consciousness
    - mental consciousness

-Finally, there is the "disturbed consciousness" that refers to the added perturbations brought to this functioning—already impure in itself—by its identification with "me" and the conflicting emotions.

PRIMORDIAL AWARENESS

As there is a potential of individualized consciousness, there is also a potential of primordial awareness. The individualized consciousness is like water polluted by mud, sand, and other impurities. Primordial awareness is the same water, but cleared of all these impurities. When one recognizes the true nature of the mind, and when this recognition is stabilized by meditation, the mind is liberated of all its defects. The potential of individualized consciousness disappears in primordial awareness. This awareness is not something that we lack now and will have to eventually acquire. We already have it right at this very moment. For example, today the sun shines in the sky, but because of the veil formed by clouds and fog, we cannot see it. When clouds and fog dissipate, we will be able to see the sun, which has always been there. In the same manner, the eight individualized consciousnesses now veil the primordial awareness for us.

The Tibetan word for Buddha is *Sang-gye*. It is composed of two syllables summarizing the essence of the Dharma. The first of the two syllables, *sang*, means "purified," referring to the fact that the mind of a Buddha is completely purified of the four veils (veils of ignorance, latent conditioning, conflicting emotions, and karma). At the same time the mode of being of the mind is revealed, inherent qualities are blossoming. This is the meaning of the second syllable, *gye*, "fully opened out." *Sang-gye*, "purified and fully opened out," gathers into two syllables all of the Dharma.

SEEING OUR FACE

Since the mind fundamentally possesses Buddha nature, one can wonder what has caused the veils to interfere. In fact, it is impossible to tell how they happened in a particular manner or at which given moment. In the same way refined gold is not found by itself in nature, but is encased in its mother rock. The purity of the mind has been covered by veils since time without beginning. Let us examine another image. Since the moment we were born from the womb of our mother, we possessed a face and a pair of eyes that allow us to see everything, except our own face. In the same way, the mind usually functions without being able to see itself. It is what is called basic ignorance.

However, there is a means that enables us to see our own face. It is sufficient to take a mirror and look at ourselves. In the spiritual domain, what can we use in place of a mirror? We have the word of the Buddha and the transmission of this word by masters. The master gives the teachings of the Buddha; the disciple listens to them, and puts them into practice. Because of that, the disciple can see his or her own face, his or her own mind.

Gampopa presented the possibility of reaching Awakening in the following way. First, all beings possess the fundamental "cause" of Awakening, which is Buddha nature. Second, the "support" which grants the ability to approach Awakening is provided by human existence; finally, the "factor" that allows us to effectively make progress on the path is the master that gives us instructions.

The path mentioned here does not mean that one must travel from one place to another, for example, leave this place to go to England. Rather, it is a transformation we must produce, transforming an impure mind into a pure mind.

A GRADUATED PATH

In this world, there are many teachings of spiritual traditions and sciences. Whatever the tradition or the science, it is impossible to become Awakened if the nature of the mind, its fundamental mode of being, is not recognized and if, consequently, one does not liberate oneself from the four veils. This requires the implementation of a graduated series of spiritual practices. First of all, one takes refuge. Then, one can engage in the practice of prostrations. This is followed by the practice of Vajrasattva (Tibetan, Dorje Sempa) which allows purification, then the offering of the *mandala*. Finally, one practices guru-yoga that opens the mind of the disciple to the grace of the master. It is then possible to accomplish profound practices such as the creation and completion phases of deity meditation, and the practice of mental calming and superior vision. Finally, one reaches mahamudra—the summit of practices. The purpose of all these methods is to dissipate the four veils and to understand the ultimate nature of the mind.

LIMITATIONS OF INFERIOR WORLDS

Allowing ourselves to be continually carried away by conflicting emotions, we accumulate negative acts which lead us to birth in inferior worlds. In hell, beings undergo extremely great torment because of intense heat or cold. Hungry ghosts, for their part, are also constantly afflicted by hunger and thirst.

Animals, which we know better, suffer from cold, from consuming each other, from being domesticated, and from having a limited intelligence. This limitation, in particular, prevents spiritual practice. A cat or a horse has few possibilities to understand what we say and even less possibility to have a spiritual practice. For example, you have a horse, a dog, or a cat that you love. If, out of this love and compassion, you patiently try to explain to your pet that it could be reborn in a pure land such as the Land of Bliss by reciting a certain number of mantras of Avalokita, the animal will not understand. If you tell your pet that it would be very beneficial to meditate even five minutes, your explanations are useless. The animal will neither understand them nor apply them. Even the best animal existence, that of domestic animals, remains an unfavorable support of existence, because it does not allow spiritual progress.

HUMAN EXISTENCE

Human existence provides the possibility of understanding the Dharma and putting it into practice. From a spiritual point of view, it is a superior existence. Nevertheless, among human beings, many have no knowledge of a spiritual path. They have no idea of what is positive or negative, what one should or should not do. They are deeply engaged in ordinary activities of this world. Many people commit many negative acts that will cause them great suffering in the future.

Most people believe they will have a long life, nevertheless few human beings become 100 years old. Death obliges all humans to leave this world one day or another, leaving behind all their material belongings. In spite of this, nearly everyone pursues temporal objectives that never exceed the framework of this present life. Among natural substances found on earth, some are considered precious, such as gold or diamonds. The human existence that is now yours is also precious. It is meaningful, because you came in contact with the Dharma, have understood it, and have met with spiritual masters.

BEFORE SUNSET

It is essential to put an authentic teaching into practice. We can do nothing without practicing. We should be able to adopt what is positive, reject what is negative, and be capable of recognizing the true nature of mind. If we receive instructions from a master and we correctly apply them, we tread a path which will lead us directly to Awakening. However, there are many people interested in the Dharma, gladly believing in its beneficial effects, but who do not make the effort to practice. In this case, how could there be benefits from the Dharma? When the sun is about to set and hides behind a high mountain, the shadow of the mountain, without anything able to stop it, spreads slowly over the plain. Our life is similar to the light that illuminates the plain. As time passes, the shadow of death grows more. We must take advantage of the years we have left to truly practice.

Most of you are young. When one is young and undertakes an activity with much ardor, there are good results. If you can put energy and force into the practice of the Dharma, you will certainly harvest good fruit. If you are older, ordinary activity in the world is nearing its end. You should be able to envisage death without fear or anguish, and prepare a happy future life continuing to walk toward liberation. To do so, it is necessary for you to devote yourself to the Dharma.

The precious human existence you now enjoy is not the fruit of randomness. It is the result of several causes, implying that in your past lives, you accumulated merit and a certain knowledge. Also, you already have made a connection with the Dharma and spiritual masters. Temporal activities have only relative importance, for, when we die, we will not be able to take anything with us. If death was the final end, and if there was nothing after this life, it would not be important to follow a spiritual path. But after this life, other existences will come, and if we do not do what is necessary for liberation, we will continue to wander endlessly in the sufferings of the cycle of existence.

NOTHING TO BE RENOUNCED

All of you this evening have a very good support of existence in this life. Some among you, perhaps the majority, have taken refuge. Taking refuge is excellent. The vows of refuge are easy to keep. They comprise no danger and because of them our positive acts become even more powerful.

Some people think that taking refuge presents a risk and some disadvantages, obligating them to reject other traditions they trust. In reality, taking refuge does not imply renouncing any other tradition. It simply means that one has confidence and engages in the Three Jewels, that is to say the Buddha, the Dharma (his teaching), and the Sangha (the community of those who transmit the teachings). Losing this confidence would break the vows of refuge. Nothing in these vows forbids one from having confidence in another tradition and its practice.

ETERNAL MIND

Our mind is not an object, having a certain color, form, matter, or volume. We can verify this by personal observation. Whether the mind does not exist as a substance and is not material, does not mean that it does not exist at all, or that it is nothingness. The proof of its existence is that it produces many thoughts and emotions, and that we feel all kinds of pleasant and unpleasant experiences. Undoubtably, most of you have studied many years and accumulated a great amount of knowledge while at school and university. This shows that the mind exists and that it does not exist materially. Indeed, let us suppose you spent 15 years in school and university. If all you learned possessed a form, it is obvious that a house could not contain it, much less your body. Because the mind is without form, and empty, it can contain everything.

As we have seen earlier, the mind is not only empty in essence, it is also clarity, and intelligence without obstruction. These are the three points defining it.

This mind, that is now ours, has existed since time without beginning. It is not born at a particular moment, it has no interruption, and it will not cease to exist. Let us take the example of space. It would be nonsense to say that it began to exist a number of years ago, or that it will disappear in so many centuries or millennia. Our mind, as immaterial as space, has no beginning and no end.

THE FUNCTIONING OF ILLUSION

If the mind is permanent, and if it has no beginning and no

end, how is it that we experience birth and death? In fact, these experiences have no reality. They are illusory productions of the mind. Let us take the example of a married couple. At first, husband and wife get along well, and are happy together. That which loves is the mind. After some time, they can no longer bear each other, they argue, and become enemies. What was joy and happiness is now transformed into suffering and enmity. This is not because the mind has become something else. The mind itself has remained the same, but its production has changed.

In general, our situation in samsara has three forms of bodily existence. In the waking state, we experience the world through our physical body, called the "fully mature karmic body." Secondly, when we sleep we live our dreams through the "body of latent conditionings." Finally, after death, and before taking birth in the *bardo*, we have a "mental body." We stay in samsara by continually taking either one or the other of these three bodies, which are accompanied by an environment of illusory projections. In the three cases, we strongly identify ourselves with what is called "I" or "me." For this "me," we want pleasant experiences in this very life; we want all that is good, and all that satisfies that "me." What we desire for this very life, we should desire much more for our lives in the future! In order to prepare for this happiness and progress on the path of liberation, there is no other way besides the Dharma.

Question: Is it absolutely necessary to have a master?
Kalu Rinpoche: A master is necessary because one cannot engage walking on a path one does not know; to know it, it is necessary for someone to teach us. We need a master, in the same sense that in school we need teachers for us to progress in our studies.

Question: Apparently some beings have reached Awakening without a master; that seems to be the case for Shakyamuni Buddha himself.
Kalu Rinpoche: One cannot say that Shakyamuni Buddha had no master. Before obtaining Awakening in Bodhgaya, he received, under the form of a mystical transmission, an ultimate initiation, that of the "great light ray," simultaneously given to him by all the Buddhas. Furthermore, in his previous lives during numerous *kalpas*, he progressed on the path by receiving the teachings of spiritual masters up to the tenth bodhisattva level. Shakyamuni Buddha, himself, said that without a spiritual master it is not possible to reach Awakening.

Question: Was Christ an authentic master and is the Christianity of today a valid tradition?
Kalu Rinpoche: I think that Christ is a completely authentic master and that his teachings have retained their value. It is said that Awakening appears under the form of numerous traditions in order to help all beings. All have value and suit different beings. This does not mean they are all identical or equal. For traveling, we have different ways of transportation. We can take a plane, a train, a car, a horse, or walk by foot; all these are ways for us to travel but not with the same speed.

I do not know Christianity well, but I think there are realized Christians. I can see that Christianity has placed a strong accent on faith and confidence, as well as emphasizing love and compassion, which is very close to Buddhism. Whatever the religion or spiritual tradition, if one studies or practices it, one can benefit from it. On the other hand, without the support of a tradition, and without receiving any teaching from a master, meditating by oneself, is like someone trying to grasp an object in complete darkness. One should not only learn theory but also put it into practice, otherwise this would hardly be beneficial. For example, if one wants to learn how to drive, it is necessary to acquire basic theoretical knowledge; but, above all, it is necessary to learn how to hold the wheel and make the car work. To practice medicine, theoretical knowledge is not enough either. It is also necessary to know how to offer health care. Suppose you are thirsty and you knew all the qualities of water. As long as you do not drink, the thirst will not be quenched. In the same way, if you know all the qualities of the Dharma but do not meditate, it will not be beneficial. Apprenticeship in the Dharma is made of three phases: first, listening, that is to say receiving knowledge; then reflecting upon it; and finally the indispensable phase of putting it into practice, which is meditating. You may know that a dish is good and very nourishing, but if you do not eat it, you will continue to be hungry.

Question: How can one help someone who is going to die?
Kalu Rinpoche: The Dharma proposes many ways to accompany dying people. Without knowing them all, one can recite the names of the Buddhas, or a mantra such as that of Avalokita in the ear of the dying person. This is extremely beneficial.

Question: Are there women who are lamas?
Kalu Rinpoche: First of all, there are some feminine deities such as Tara, Vajrayogini, and others. Moreover, during the history of Tibet, many masters were women. Some have remained famous, like Machik Labdron or Yeshe Tsogyal. Whether a man or a woman, one possesses a mind, and consequently, the potential for Awakening. It is said that the essence of all beings is Buddha nature; it is not said that the essence of all male beings is the Buddha.

Question: What benefit are the mantras?
Kalu Rinpoche: If we have confidence in the mantra we recite, the spiritual force, the force of compassion with which it is charged, allows us to establish our mind in emptiness.

Brussels, October 1984

Bodhgaya Teaching

This teaching and the two that follow are the last teachings given by Kalu Rinpoche. They are, in some way, his spiritual will. Staying for the last time in Bodhgaya, where the Buddha attained Awakening, Kalu Rinpoche addressed a group of Westerners, many of whom were his close disciples. He gave a summary of his approach to Buddhism, which was almost elliptic at times. He also made an assessment of his activity in the West.

A SITUATION SO DIFFICULT TO OBTAIN

The existence given us in this present life represents an exceptionally favorable situation. It is difficult to be born in the place where we are, the "continent of the South," "Jambudvipa".[35] It is difficult to acquire what we have obtained, the precious human existence endowed with the 18 freedoms and qualifications. It is difficult to meet that with which we have made contact, the teaching of the Buddha and authentic spiritual masters. Finally, it is difficult to have the opportunity to hear what we have heard, the instructions of the Small Vehicle, the Great Vehicle, and the Vajrayana delivered by the Buddha.

We have, during our life, the choice of two paths: the spiritual way and the temporal way. The temporal way allows us to obtain happiness, well-being, success, wealth, fame, or power, in the framework of our present existence. The spiritual way leads us to mastering our mind by the

---

[35]In the traditional Buddhist cosmology, the universe is composed of an axial mountain surrounded by four "continents," among them, to the South, is "Jambudvipa" corresponding to our planet Earth.

knowledge of its nature and, ultimately, allows us to reach Buddhahood. Of these two paths, the spiritual path is the more important.

LET US MEASURE OUR GOOD FORTUNE

We have now obtained human existence. If this were not so, and, for example, we were born as a god, our wealth, pleasures, and happiness would be so great that we would spend a lifetime enjoying them, unmotivated to turn away from the cycle of existences. We would not have the opportunity of following the spiritual path. If we were born as a demi-god, the consequences of our past actions engendering this type of rebirth would have given way to jealousy and pugnacity as virulent as a devouring fire, so we could not possibly have the opportunity of following a spiritual path.

We could have been born in hell where beings suffer from extreme heat and cold; in the world of the hungry ghosts tormented by intense hunger and thirst; or again in the world of animals with a limited intelligence who suffer having to hunt and consume each other in order to survive. In all these states of existence, even if we heard some teachings, we would perceived the words without understanding their meaning.

A CITY WOULD SUFFICE

On our planet, there are many countries, large and small, where human beings are continually born. However, not all follow a spiritual path. Most of them have no previous connection with the Dharma, nor aspiration to discover it. If one were to gather all the inhabitants of this world into 100 cities, a single city would suffice to contain those who practice a spiritual path. If all the inhabitants of this city were involved people, it would be wonderful! Many are content with the external appearance of practice. Those who take their spiritual life seriously are as rare as stars during the day. You have entered the path, you have confidence and you try to make progress. This is a sign of a good connection in the past and a good aspiration in the present.

MYSTERY OF CONNECTIONS

You were born in different countries of the world where the teaching of the Buddha is largely unknown. However, at adulthood you have become interested in Buddhism. You have received instructions and decided to apply them. You have studied, your confidence has grown, and you have practiced with joy. This turn in your existence implies that, sometime, during your past lives, you practiced generosity, ethics, patience, diligence, concentration, and transcendental knowledge. In this manner you practiced the six paramitas as well as positive acts. You also certainly have had a particular connection with the Buddha, his teaching, and the Buddhist community.

An idea has occurred to me on this point. The Buddha, his teaching, and the community manifest a great force of compassion and blessing. When I was a child, my parents had a deep confidence in the Three Jewels. As soon as I was of an age to understand, I heard about the Buddha, the Dharma, the Sangha and lamas, and I have felt an extraordinary faith in them. At a very young age, I felt an unusual and intense love and compassion toward animals. Because of my faith, I recited the names of the Buddhas and mantras such as OM MANI PADME HUNG to all the insects, animals and birds that I met. To offer them something, I gave them food blended with consecrated substances. Then, I recited this prayer: "When liberated of this miserable existence, may you be born as human in the next life. May I be able to help you enter the Dharma and attain Awakening." I also fed consecrated substances mixed with tsampa[36] to fish, ants, and other small animals, praying for their happiness.

Later, as an old man, I traveled to foreign countries. I do not know foreign languages, only Tibetan, my mother tongue; yet many people seemed happy to meet me and follow my teachings. Sometimes, I wonder if these beings are not the same ones whom, a long time ago, I helped and protected by reciting the names of the Buddhas and prayers.

I cannot be sure of that, having no direct vision of it, but I do not believe this is impossible. Nowadays, there are many younger *tulkus*, more attractive, and better educated than I. Despite this, many people are seemingly attracted to me. I believe those who come to me were born in present circumstances because of the activity of the mantras and prayers I recited for them a long time ago.

VASUBANDHU'S PIGEONS

How is this possible? Long ago in India there lived a master called Vasubandhu, a disciple of Asanga. He lived in a house that sheltered many pigeons under its roof. When he was home, Vasubandhu recited discourses of the Buddha aloud. Every day, he offered water and seeds to the spirits. When it was done, he threw the seeds through the door. The birds heard the chanted texts and ate the scattered seeds. After their death, they were born as disciples of Vasubandhu. One became even more learned than his master in the domain of the sutras; another more expert in the texts treating monastic discipline. In their past lives, all of them were none other than the pigeons nesting under the awnings. Such a connection between facts may appear inconceivable to us; nevertheless, it is quite possible if one refers to the law of karmic connection.

---

[36]Flour of roasted barley.

EMPTY-HANDED

It would be a great loss not to practice the spiritual way and instead exclusively devote ourselves to temporal activities. Even if those brought us power, force, wealth, attraction, and well-being, our unavoidable death will leave us alone and empty-handed, as if we wakened from a dream. In a long term perspective, they appear neither necessary nor useful. While dying, we will take away nothing other than the mind and the positive or negative karma we have accumulated during our lifetime.

INNER AND OUTER DISCIPLINE

Buddhist discipline can be seen as having two sides, inner and outer. Renouncing the ten negative acts[37] and practicing the ten positive acts[38] are part of the outer teachings. Because of the law of karma, and by adopting this conduct, we will no longer undergo the pain and suffering of inferior existence in our future lives. The ten positive acts will allow us to obtain a comfortable, pleasant, long, and happy existence in the world of human beings or gods.

Inner teachings comprise the respect of different vows: the vows of individual liberation, bodhisattva vows, and sacred commitments of the Vajrayana. They also concern the "phases of creation and completion" of the meditation, as well as meditation on compassion and emptiness, which lead to recognition of the ultimate nature of the mind. We then reach different stages of liberation from the first to the tenth levels

---

[37]The ten negative acts are: killing, stealing, sexual misconduct, lying, creating discord, using harsh words, meaningless talk, envy, ill will, and wrong views.

[38]The ten positive acts are: protecting life, giving, having a moral conduct, speaking truthfully, reconciling others, speaking gently, talking mindfully, being content, benefiting others, and abandoning wrong views.

of the bodhisattva, and finally, complete Awakening—free of all suffering.

LISTENING, REFLECTING, AND MEDITATING

Practicing the teachings of the Buddha offers two advantages, a temporal benefit, obtaining fortunate conditions of existence, and an ultimate benefit—liberation. It is necessary to get a solid foundation by correctly listening, reflecting, and meditating. We must begin by listening[39] to the teachings, that is to have some knowledge of them. We reflect on what we have studied until convinced of its validity. Finally, after having understood the meaning of the teachings, we meditate, taking them as the basis of our meditation. When these three steps, listening, reflecting, and meditating, are correctly done, our practice automatically becomes efficient and beneficial. If we begin to practice Buddhism without listening, studying, or reflecting, we will have an insufficient and superficial comprehension that produces a practice that is not correct, authentic, or beneficial.

Let us take an example. The teachings of the Buddha inform us that the human existence is characterized by sufferings due to birth, sickness, old age, and death. From listening, we obtain some knowledge of this. We then reflect on these different types of suffering. Becoming aware of what they are, we begin to see that we have to live in a way to rid ourselves of them in this and future lives. We will decide to realize the nature of mind, beyond birth and death, beyond all suffering. Having passed this step of reflecting, we undertake the practice of meditation in order to reach liberation.

---

[39]The term "listening," in this context, means "to be informed, having knowledge"; therefore, it refers not only to the effective listening of oral teachings, but also to the reading of authentic texts.

PRECIOUS HUMAN EXISTENCE

If we follow the instructions of a lama, first, we will be taught the ten qualifications and the eight freedoms of the precious human existence that we possess now. The difficulty of obtaining this life will be explained through "causes, numbers and metaphors."[40]

The "causes" refer to obtaining a precious human existence. It is necessary to have practiced the ten positive acts and abandoned the ten negative acts in our past lives. The being who has not acted in this way cannot enjoy all the freedoms and qualifications which make human life to be the precious human life. There are few who observe right ethics, and are able to be born in these favorable conditions.

The "numbers" refer to the small proportion of human beings compared to those in other conditions of existence. For example, we see that a relatively large number of people reside between Bodhgaya, where we are, and the neighboring city of Gaya. The number of insects living underground in this area is without doubt 100 times, perhaps 1,000 or 100,000 times greater than the number of human beings. Comparatively, the number of humans is relatively small. Likewise, compared to animals, hungry ghosts are even far more numerous. If we reflect on it, we will come to think: "Now, I have obtained human birth. If I do not give meaning to this life by following a spiritual path, this opportunity will be ruined."

---

[40]Kalu Rinpoche will explain the "causes" and the "numbers." He does not talk about "metaphors." Metaphors are traditional comparisons showing the rarity of precious human existence. The best known is the metaphor of a blind tortoise living at the bottom of an ocean which surfaces through a floating gold covered ring. The tortoise only reaches the surface once in every 100 years; it is said that the tortoise is more likely to pass its neck through the ring than for a being in samsara to obtain a precious human existence.

A SOLID FOUNDATION

It is necessary to reflect on the impermanence of our human existence. Our life can be reduced to a succession of years, months, days, hours, or even seconds. Like the flow of a large river, our life is impermanent, and changes from instant to instant until death. After this, life ends and we no longer can make any use of it. When we meditate on death, we understand it is necessary to use the time we have left to study authentic spiritual teachings.

When we think of the suffering in the cycle of existences, we become convinced that we must avoid this rebirth, so we study the means for this, that is, the teachings of the Buddha.

Finally, by studying the law of karma, we understand that positive acts are the cause of happiness, and negative acts the cause of suffering. We are led to accomplish positive activity and to avoid the negative. By a progressive approach, we assimilate the teachings of the Buddha. We reflect upon them, and then we meditate. Doing this, we are sure to establish an authentic and correct spiritual practice.

VARIOUS VEHICLES

We can practice the Small Vehicle, the Great Vehicle, or the Vajrayana.

By practicing the Small Vehicle, we become aware of the cycle of existences—an ocean of suffering. We see that this cycle creates suffering, and it is impermanent by nature and we turn away from it. Following the directives of our master, we learn to meditate by concentrating on the emptiness of the individual. Through meditation, we overcome our enemies which are our own conflicting emotions. This results in the path of the "listeners," called "the victory over the enemies" (the state of *arhat*). Going beyond the simple emptiness of the mind, one then meditates on the emptiness of all animate and inanimate phenomena; one reaches the realization of a "solitary Buddha." Listeners and solitary Buddhas are in the framework of the Small Vehicle.

We arrive at an understanding of our own emptiness and that of others because of the instructions of our master. In fact, we see that suffering has no own existence, and we develop compassion for all beings. Not perceiving this emptiness, beings are attached to the appearances of samsara and their suffering never ends. Great compassion toward beings is linked to meditation on emptiness. From here, we enter the path of the bodhisattva. The Great Vehicle puts in practice the six perfections, which are generosity, ethics, patience, diligence, concentration, and transcendent knowledge, keeping as a foundation the union of emptiness and compassion. By this path, the practitioner reaches the first level of the bodhisattva, then passes through the levels that lead to the tenth stage.

FROM IMPURE TO PURE

As long as we have not realized the nature of our mind we remain ordinary beings. Our consciousness is not at one with innate primordial awareness. It is an impure individual consciousness that makes us perceive phenomena in a dualistic mode. Forms, sounds, tastes, contacts with earth, water, fire, air, and space in the external world are on one side, and on the other—our flesh, blood, breath, bones and articulations, nervous system, pores of our skin, and so on, in our body. Their totality falls into groups which are the aggregates, elements and senses, and become the source of suffering.

Each of these groups contains a certain number of aspects. One example is the enumeration of five aggregates: forms, sensations, perceptions, volitions, and consciousnesses. All are supports for suffering, in which one can say that "suffering is inherent in all compounded phenomena."

Suffering comes from an impure mind. When we study the teachings of the Buddha and put them in practice, we understand that this impure mind, as "potential of individual consciousness" (Sanskrit, *alayavijnana*), is comparable to muddy water. Pure and clear water corresponds to the realization of the nature of the mind, and is referred to as the "potential of primordial awareness" (Sanskrit, *alayajnana*). From the point of primordial awareness, the five elements of the external world (earth, water, fire, air, and space) are perceived as the five feminine Buddhas. The five aggregates (forms, sensations, perceptions, volitions, and consciousnesses) are the five masculine Buddhas. The five conflicting emotions (desire, anger, mental opacity, pride, and jealousy) are the five wisdoms. All negative aspects of our experience become positive. All appearances are transmuted and realized as the nature of Buddhas and bodhisattvas, divine and pure appearances. It is why the "wisdom deities," Buddhas and bodhisattvas truly exist.

Buddhas and bodhisattvas have given human beings teachings that constitute a treasury of instructions shared today by many masters. If we receive initiations and instructions from these masters, we will be able, by practicing meditation, to accomplish the transmutation of the potential of individual consciousness into the potential of primordial awareness. In the Vajrayana, one uses techniques including visualizations of deities, recitations of mantras, meditative absorption states, and *mudras*. With these means we can hope to reach Awakening in this very life, like Marpa, Milarepa, Gampopa, or Khyungpo Naljor.

THE GOOD PEASANT

Since 1971, I have traveled to many countries in the world, from north to south, east to west. I have given many initiations, explained the Dharma, and given instructions. I have created retreat centers and Dharma centers. I have spread the teachings of the Buddha using various methods. It can be said that I am a peasant who has planted his field well. Many other lamas and tulkus of the Sakyapa, Gelukpa, Kagyupa, and Nyingmapa traditions of Tibetan Buddhism have undertaken similar work, so that Buddhism now has spread within most countries of the world. Seeds have been planted well.

The real fruit that can be expected from this is that many people achieve the three-year and three-month retreat. However, with rare exceptions, the result did not meet what was expected, because many entered the retreat in a rush, without having sufficiently studied and understood the teachings of the Buddha. Their meditation during the retreat has not been as fruitful as we were expecting, because of this insufficient preparation and understanding. Have they made progress on the path of Awakening? The results are uncertain, and do not meet all the criteria of progress. Therefore, I cannot tell if my projects have truly been accomplished.

For this reason, I have formed a translation committee in charge of The Treasury of Knowledge.[41] I feel that this is an efficient way to remedy the situation. When this encyclopedia is translated into several languages, people interested in Buddhism will be able to reach a better understanding. Those who have already practiced in Buddhist centers, or who have accomplished the three-year and three-month retreat will be able to deepen their experience and understanding of meditation. They also will be able to immediately harvest the fruits of their practice. At least, this is my hope.

Bodhgaya, 1989

---

[41]This Treasury of Knowledge, that is to say an encyclopedia of Buddhism and traditional sciences linked with it, is a compilation undertaken by Lodro Thaye, one of the most remarkable Tibetan masters of the nineteenth century. The English translation is currently being worked on.

Vasubandhu

The Next to the Last Teaching

The Buddha gave 84,000 teachings for the benefit of all beings that are included in the three approaches, or vehicles of Hinayana, Mahayana, and Vajrayana. In the present age, it is through these forms that the Dharma spreads throughout the world. This is the case with the Tibetan tradition, in particular, which is based on the collection of these three vehicles. From any one of these approaches, what matters is to overcome schemes fabricated with the samsaric mind, an ego-structured mind that looks after its own interests or profit, and tries to gain richness, fame, and so on, for itself. Hinayana, Mahayana, and Vajrayana reject such an attitude. It is important to renounce this egotistical attitude of samsara.

THE THREE VEHICLES

From the Hinayana point of view, it is the strong fixation on oneself that creates ego—the source of the 84,000 disturbing emotions of our mind; pleasure, displeasure, indifference, inferior and superior states of consciousness—all the sufferings of samsara originate with this fixation. Hinayana teaches how to overcome the fixation of ego by meditation on transcendent knowledge of non-ego.

In Mahayana one is not only concerned with one's own liberation from the fixation of ego, but with the liberation of all beings from the suffering of samsara and helping them to attain the perfect joy of Awakening. The practices of Mahayana and Hinayana aim at overcoming the compulsive attitudes of attraction, repulsion, and indifference, linked with ego.

The area of concern in Vajrayana, as in Hinayana and Mahayana, is overcoming the fixation of ego. One must liberate oneself from attachments, repulsions, and indifference. The feeling of existing, the thought, "I am, I have a body," and the experience of what we usually consider to be real—all that we can be attached to, the fixations of dualistic grasping—must be completely overcome. To liberate oneself from these fixations, Vajrayana employs methods such as meditation on a deity and recitation of the deity's mantra.

A DIVIDED LIFE

By previous connections with the Three Jewels and the merit accumulated in past existences, you have obtained a precious human existence. Because of the kindness of the lama, your spiritual friend, you can understand many teachings even if you cannot understand all of the Dharma. This is important because, today, there are many practitioners of Dharma aspiring to Buddhahood but who have not yet overcome the fixations of ego! They continue to cultivate thoughts and desires such as, "I must have happiness, pleasure, success. I have to be known in the world. I have to be wealthy. I have to have this and that, and so on." All these ideas come from fixations and attachments.

I also see many people who practice at times with the mind of Dharma, and then again with the mind of samsara. Sometimes the Dharma viewpoint is dominant and at other times samsara predominates. So goes their life. Sometimes they practice the Dharma, but sometimes they forget. To practice Dharma it is necessary to recognize the essence of mind and practice what is really useful to it. That means practicing that which will diminish the disturbing emotions—desire, aversion, ignorance, pride, jealousy, and avarice. And then, practicing that which will completely liberate us from them. If one acts in this way, one truly practices the Dharma.

CULTURAL CONTEXTS

All practitioners, Westerners and Easterners, are fundamentally in the same situation, sharing the precious human existence and the benefits that come from circumstances that are favorable to the authentic practice of Dharma. However, there are some dissimilarities in their approaches that come from differences engendered by their respective cultures. Easterners have a familiarity with the Dharma that allows them an affinity with it. For them, the teachings are obviously true and they think it is good to practice and meditate on them. They easily and naturally recite mantras, do prostrations, circumambulations and make traditional offerings of butter lamps, and so on. They have, because of their cultural background, a feeling that these practices are positive even if there are few who understand the reason. Some meditate deeply. Even those who do not know how to meditate have a positive relation with the teachings. This enables them to recite billions of mantras such as OM MANI PADME HUNG or to do many times 100,000 recitations of the 100 syllable mantra of Vajrasattva. They also engage in Dharma activities such as the making of *tsa-tsa* (types of miniature stupas) or other things. All these activities are very positive and useful for practice.

In the West, the introduction of Dharma is recent. With respect to Vajrayana, particularly recent. There is no cultural background. Generally Westerners have good karmic connection with the Dharma. They appreciate it and consider its teachings to be true. They also have confidence that is not connected to a cultural past, and because of this they are mainly attracted by meditation. This is good, although they are reluctant to do other activities such as recitation of mantras. Even when they understand some Dharma, there are few who will recite the *manis*, the Thirty-Five Buddhas Confession Prayer, or the Prayer of the Activities of Samantabhadra. The Buddha taught that these practices are very positive. This attitude on their part is formed by lack of confidence in the Buddha, and absence of previous habits and cultural background. In fact, these different activities of the Dharma bring great benefits and the Buddha taught them in order to help us. There are benefits from meditation, pujas, prostrations, circumambulations, and all the practices that purify body and speech. It is not a matter of one approach being right and the other wrong. They all bring similar benefits.

INVESTING YOURSELF COMPLETELY

One who receives the teachings and practices them is a human being made up of body, speech, and mind. These human elements at first seem to be radically different, but they fundamentally belong together and are interdependent. Without speech, the body would not know how to express itself, and without body, there would be no speech. The practice of Dharma concerns our whole being; this means our body, speech, and mind. There are positive and negative acts of body, speech, and mind. Likewise, the accumulation of merit and purification practices deal with all aspects of our being. All these practices and teachings of the Buddha are useful in the attainment of Awakening. Whatever time you can commit to the practice of Dharma—be it one year, one month, one week, or one day—the motivation is extremely important. It should be done with bodhicitta, the mind of Awakening. This means telling yourself that you are going to do it for the benefit of all beings. Having this inner attitude as the basis of all practices is very important. While progressing on the path, the most important thing, if one can do it, is to understand, as much as possible, the nature of the mind. Each practice should be done with this understanding as a basis.

ESSENCE OF THE TEACHING

If one can do recitations and physical practices with speech and body while meditating on the nature of mind, these will bring even greater benefit. To truly understand the nature of mind is very delicate. To arrive at this, a lama must give us instructions over a long period of time, and then we ourselves have to meditate a long time on these instructions, examining the mind accordingly. Deep devotion to the lama as well as practices of accumulation and purification are very important. Without the conjunction of these elements, it is difficult to recognize the nature of mind.

For this recognition, it is necessary to have both a realized lama with authentic capabilities, and a disciple qualified by devotion with previous accumulation of merit and purification. When such a meeting occurs, the lama can uncover the superior capabilities of the disciple, and this disciple will be receptive to the lama's teachings. The lama can guide the disciple, directly pointing out the fundamental state of mind to him. The disciple then will meditate within this understanding. Everything is included in this practice; there is no need for anything else. Today it is rare to meet such a qualified lama or disciple. There are few lamas who teach in this way. Therefore, it is important that I talk to you about it. I am old, my body is no longer in good shape. We will not be together much longer. In this brief time, I wish to speak about what can help you. To teach you many things would not be useful.

MIND BEYOND NAMING

What is the nature of our mind? "Mind" is a word. Besides this word, this appellation, there is nothing that one can use as a basis for designation, nothing of which one can say, "This is it." The mind has no form, no color; nothing can identify it. It is called emptiness.

This emptiness of mind is undefinable, like space but not inert and obscure emptiness. It is not lacking awareness, because if this were the case, the mind could not produce anything and would not be of any use.

The nature of this emptiness is luminosity. This means a lucidity tending toward awareness. This emptiness and luminosity are not two different things. They are undifferentiated. Properly speaking, there is the intelligence and the aspects of its awareness. One calls it *shepa* or *rigpa* and without doubt, the best term is *rigpa*. Therefore, the nature of the mind is emptiness-luminosity-awareness, the three cannot be separated. This is what one gives for the name of mind. If we look for our mind, we will not find it. However, one should observe it, otherwise it cannot be known.

In what way should it be observed? By letting it be without either restraint or artifice (*dzo chu me pa*) in its natural state. This meditation proves to be very delicate because when one leaves the mind in its natural state, if the mind is lacking lucidity, it is useless. It is then simply a state of stupidity that has nothing to do with meditation. However, if one meditates properly, then, through natural progression, one will recognize the nature of mind and understand what it is. But this practice poses a problem.

WHAT METHOD TO CHOOSE?

Since the beginning of our existence in samsara up to now, we have never known how to leave our mind at rest. It is constantly agitated by innumerable thoughts. They are like waves continually appearing on the surface of the ocean of mind. They never cease.

It is necessary to learn how to leave the mind at rest. To do this, there are the practices of *shinay* (*shinay* literally means to "stay tranquil"). There are many types of *shinay* that use various means, some are meditations on emptiness; others use supports such as luminous points (*tigle*), and so on. Whatever type of *shinay*, one must practice it for a long time—months, years—if not, the mind cannot rest. This practice of *shinay* must not be mixed with mental opaqueness. If it is, one might spend a whole lifetime without any result. This is another difficulty in the practice!

AVALOKITA PRACTICE

The best practice, gathering the most advantages, is the meditation of Chenrezig.[42] A saying that comes from the teaching of Chenrezig is, "The one who meditates on Chenrezig or simply keeps him present in the mind purifies limitless negative actions. Meditating on Chenrezig or simply keeping him present in the mind has the power to purify the most negative actions especially those that have immediate consequences." This was taught by the Great Compassionate One himself.

Meditating on Chenrezig, reciting his mantra, and in this practice, meditating on the nature of mind, purifies negative karma accumulated for innumerable aeons. While doing this purification, one cannot miss recognizing the nature of mind. This takes place naturally. In the meditation of Chenrezig, we begin by simply meditating that "We are Chenrezig" while continually reciting the mantra (either with a *mala* that joins movement and speech, or without a *mala*—both are possible). At the beginning, it might be difficult to meditate that one is Chenrezig with all his attributes. If one cannot see him clearly, it does not matter. It is sufficient to simply meditate, thinking that one is truly Chenrezig. With more familiarity with the practice, one will form an increasingly clear image of him. Meditation like this on oneself as the body of Chenrezig, an empty appearance (Tibetan, *nang tong*) like a rainbow, one

---

[42]Practice of Chenrezig was continually recommended by Kalu Rinpoche and he frequently gave Chenrezig initiation. For more details on the practice, the reader can refer to *Chenrezig, Lord of Love* by Bokar Rinpoche (ClearPoint Press).

leaves the mind at rest without distraction. In this state one recites as many *manis* as one can. It is when one meditates like this that the practice of *shinay* develops naturally and progressively. Then, from time to time, one leaves the mind in the presence of Chenrezig, relaxed, lucid, without artifice, simply dwelling in his presence. One remains like that as long as one can. This aspect of the practice is very useful in approaching the practice of mahamudra.

Sometimes, while continually reciting *manis*, one leaves the mind in the simple experience of the mantric sound without thinking, "This is good, this is bad, this is strong, this is slow, this is great, this is small or whatever." This is an excellent means to develop *shinay*. These different practices are not only means to develop *shinay*, because if one keeps in mind the form of Chenrezig or the sound of the mantra, at the same time one is practicing *shinay*, the presence of Chenrezig in the mind has the power to purify aeons of negative karma.

We are beginners and our ability to leave the mind without artifice while simply reciting OM MANI PADME HUNG is perhaps limited. If this is the case, one can also, without reciting *manis*, simply leave the mind at rest without artifice as long as one can. From time to time, one can also turn with confidence toward Lama Chenrezig and develop compassion for all beings. Then, one addresses the Lama Chenrezig with the prayer requesting that we all realize mahamudra. Praying in this way, again and again, is very important. At the end of the meditation, one dedicates the benefit of the practice to all beings and makes positive wishes. This should be done at the end of every Dharma practice.

PRELIMINARY PRACTICES

Besides the meditation of Chenrezig, one can do the practices that are the preliminary to mahamudra. In the practice of prostrations, one meditates that the space in front of oneself is completely filled with all the aspects of refuge. One develops great trust and devotion toward them. With the body one does prostrations, with the speech recites the words of refuge, and with the mind engenders trust and devotion.

When we do the recitation of the 100 syllable mantra, the Lama Vajrasattva is on the top of our head. We request him to purify all of the negative actions and veils that we have accumulated since time without beginning. Meditating like this, one recites the mantra. Nectar flows from his body, filling the inside of our own body, purifying all the negative actions and veils, and flows out of us in the form of black liquid. At the end of this purification, body, speech, and mind of the Lama Vajrasattva and our own body, speech, and mind, become undifferentiated.

When we do the offering of *mandala*, we meditate that in the space in front of us, there truly are the Three Jewels and Three Roots. We offer them all of what is beautiful and agreeable such as forms, sounds, smells, tastes, and touch. We fill all the universes without limit and meditate that they are completely filled by these offerings.

When we do the practice of *guru yoga*, (Tibetan, *lama naljor*), we meditate on our root lama. This means the one who gave us initiations, instructions, transmission, and who, by the connection we have with him, is the most useful for our mind. We imagine him in the aspect of Vajradhara. His appearance is that of Vajradhara, but in essence it is the root lama himself. The Buddha Vajradhara is surrounded by all the lamas of the lineage—all those who have transmitted the teachings since the lineage's origin. We develop trust and devotion toward them and recite the six verses. Their meaning is that of a prayer, requesting that they grant us the realization of mahamudra. At the end, we receive the four initiations, then the mind of the lama and our mind melt together. Well, there is enough teaching. Now, it is appropriate you practice as much as you can!

Sonada, March-April 1989

Yeshe Tsogyal

The Last Public Teaching

COMMUNICATION LIMITS

The totality of space is permeated by beings who experience the six different realms of existence. Some can see all the forms of animate life; others have no power to see beings of another realm. The beings of hell and hungry ghosts are the most miserable. For extremely long periods, the beings of the hell realm suffer from extremes of heat and cold; hungry ghosts experience great hunger and thirst. If we were able to see them, we would feel pity and compassion and think that it is absolutely necessary to do something to help them. We are not able to see these realms, nor are beings in those realms able to see us. Our only source for understanding their condition is the description of these realms that is contained in the Buddha's teachings. Apart from practicing the teachings, there is no way for us to help these beings.

Among the beings we are able to see in this world, there are the various species of animals including birds, cows, dogs, cats, pigs, goats, sheep, frogs, insects, and so on. We are able to perceive the great sufferings they undergo and the inherent limitations in their lives that prevent them from ending their suffering. If we wish to help them by speaking to them about Dharma, it will have no effect as they cannot understand our words and cannot practice. Although reciting the names of Buddhas, mantras, or long mantras called *dharanis* in the range of their hearing offers some help, we are unable to be of great benefit to them.

Those to whom we are able to communicate the meaning of the Dharma and have an expectation of their understanding, and benefitting from it, are the human beings of this world. Few people can understand the Dharma. Perhaps 99 percent of humanity does not understand. Some of those who know a little Dharma have no interest in it; others have absolutely no faith in the Dharma, no matter what anyone might say. Because most people fall into this category, except for the one out of a hundred who appreciates the import of the Dharma, it is difficult for us to help others through Dharma teachings.

There are a few people who understand the teachings of Buddha, who trust them, and who have entered the path of Buddhist practice. For those who have the good fortune to meet the Dharma, it is most beneficial and important to understand, study, and energetically practice it during this lifetime.

UNDERSTANDING MIND

The mind is the root of understanding for practicing the Dharma. It is the mind that wanders throughout samsara. It is mind that experiences sufferings. It is mind that transcends suffering, that is to say, attains the state of Buddhahood, and then works for the benefit of all beings. Apart from mind there is nothing else whatsoever in samsara or nirvana. It is most important for us to understand mind.

Let us take an example of water mixed with earth. This muddy water is not useful to us, but the same water, when its impurities are eliminated, is clear, pure, and useful for drinking, boiling for tea, and so forth. Our mind in its gross state is like muddy water, and is called the potential of individual consciousness (*alayavijnana*). The mind in its natural purity is like clear water, the potential of primordial awareness (*alayajnana*).

If we understand the nature of mind to some extent, we naturally comprehend karma, the workings of action, cause, and effect. As a result, we give up all negative actions and the sufferings they cause, and then act virtuously, thus creating good karma. Let us consider more closely this link between the understanding of mind and the comprehension of karma.

FORCE OF KARMA

To begin with, impure mind is the potential of individualized consciousness (*alayavijnana*) that is like earth. It has the characteristics of the earth element, solidity and compactness. It is also moist, showing presence of the water element. Its warmth is the fire element; its movement, the wind element; its spacious quality—providing support for lakes, trees, grass, and so on—the element of space. Therefore, potential of individualized consciousness, like earth, contains all five elements. From it appears the "collection of the eight consciousnesses." These are the potential of individualized consciousness itself plus the ego consciousness and the six sense consciousnesses: visual, auditory, olfactory, gustatory, tactile, and mental consciousness. The "five aggregates" that make up individuality and other aspects of our experience also appear. Experiences of the ordinary mind develop from these latent potentialities in the potential of individualized consciousness. These experiences are conditioned by and grow from karmic imprints that are also latent in the potential of individualized consciousness; it is the container and source of all karmic factors. Causes and effects of karma are planted in the earth of this potential of individualized consciousness, they grow, and bear fruit. The events of samsara also come from this potential of individualized consciousness.

Karmic causes are created by disturbing emotions. For example, if we have a particular possession, we think, "This is mine." In this way, we develop attachment toward it. If we worry about others possessing it, we become greedy. This feeling of greed is a cause, that, once "dissolved" into or imprinted upon the potential of individualized consciousness, results in poverty, loss, and increased greed. In the same way, positive and negative causes produce corresponding results.

The principal teaching of the Buddha is said to be the action, cause, and effect, of karma. The reason for this is that by behaving correctly in terms of action, cause, and effect, harmful actions toward oneself and others diminish, and virtue increases. It is thereby possible for us to gather the accumulations of merit and wisdom, and ultimately to attain Buddhahood.

VEHICLES AND PATHS

The first step on this path to Awakening is to take refuge in the Three Jewels, Buddha, Dharma, and Sangha. Then, one reflects upon karma, action, cause, and effect. The path of accumulation is abandoning negative actions, and acting virtuously according to one's understanding. On this basis, we start to develop compassion, meditation, trust, and the practice of a *yidam*, and so on. These practices are the first step on the path called "the path of accumulation." This path has three levels: lesser, medium, and highest. These levels depend on the accumulation of merit and primordial awareness. All these positive qualities continue to grow and transcendental knowledge develops. At that point, the path of integration has been reached. It is called the path of integration because it occurs before the next stage, the path of seeing by which one is able to contemplate the nature of mind. Before this stage, the nature of mind has been contemplated intellectually and not directly experienced.

The path of integration also has three levels. If one continues to meditate with energy, one passes these levels. When one really understands the nature of mind, this is the moment of entering the path of seeing.

Development through the lesser, middle, and highest levels of the path of seeing continues until its culmination on the highest level. At that point, the nature of mind—the union of emptiness, clarity, and unobstructed awareness—is seen as we might recognize a close friend. The paths of accumulation, integration, and seeing, are each made of three levels: lesser, middle, and highest. They are integral to the Hinayana, Mahayana, and Vajrayana alike. The three yanas are three different vehicles, or means, to travel on the same path. These vehicles are different presentations of the Buddha's teaching that help us travel in the same direction. Each of the three yanas is a source of great spiritual influence and excellent compassion. There is no difference between them in that they are all means to reach the different spiritual levels.

There is, however, a great difference in the length of these paths. Hinayana is a very long path; Mahayana is more direct; the Vajrayana is the shortest path of all. For example, it is explained that for a being of the highest capability, Vajrayana leads to Awakening in this lifetime; for someone of average capability, in the period between death and rebirth in the *bardo*; and for someone of lesser capability, after three or seven lifetimes of practice. Therefore, from the perspective of Vajrayana practice, the paths of accumulation, integration, and seeing, are short. Because the Vajrayana has skillful means and great compassion that enrich its practice, our present opportunity to practice it is most fortunate.

MULTIPLICATION OF EFFECTS

To illustrate this point, the Buddha said there is nothing more beneficial than the recitation of the mantra OM MANI PADME HUNG. A person wishing to recite one hundred million of these mantras might approach this in a Hinayana way by reciting the mantras alone. If one is diligent, it would take over three years for the recitation to be completed. In a Mahayana style, one would assemble several people who could recite the mantra. The mantras recited by each member of the group are all added together. This is a much faster way of completing the sum but it would still demand a long time.

From a Vajrayana perspective, however, one would meditate with stability, imagining ten thousand or one hundred thousand emanations of oneself as Chenrezig, and think that they are all actually present, continually reciting the mantras. If this practice is done with faith, the total would be completed in a matter of hours or days. The various vehicles have these kinds of differences in efficacy.

If we have great faith in a particular lama, *yidam*, or Buddha, and we wish to do one hundred thousand prostrations to him or her, it would take a long time. The practice of taking refuge in one figure alone will remove negative karma and gather some merit. However, in our practice of the four foundations, we might imagine the sky before us filled with lamas, *yidams*, Buddhas, bodhisattvas, *dakinis*, protectors, and guardians of the Dharma and meditate that they really manifest before us. If we imagine that we are sending thousands, hundreds of thousands of emanations of our bodies that, together with all beings, prostrate before them, we accumulate limitless merit and also remove countless obscurations. This is practice done according to the Vajrayana path.

Similarly, a wealthy person might have gold or silver, precious stones, silk, or a valuable possession and decides to use it to accomplish merit by offering it to a lama or Buddha in whom he or she has faith. The person might present it to the lama or Buddha saying, "This is precious to me; I'd like you to have it." Making such a pure offering is very wonderful and is a means for accumulating great merit. However, there is a method in the Vajrayana path to make offerings; it is the *mandala* offering. During this meditation, we continually offer our body, speech, mind, worldly possessions; virtue accumulated in the past, present, or future; the enjoyments of gods and humans—beautiful forms and sounds, delicious tastes and smells, and pleasing sensations—to the Buddhas and bodhisattvas of the ten directions. We offer again and again, with an attitude of great faith and thereby accumulate thousands, ten thousands, hundreds of thousands times more merit than the offering described earlier and the purification of negative karma is proportionate to the accumulation of merit.

WEARING SHOES

The path of Vajrayana is endowed with infinite skillful means that make it a very quick path. What is the source of these skillful means of the Vajrayana? They come from mind itself. If we understand that all phenomena arise from mind and its nature is emptiness, clarity, and unimpeded awareness, we will understand that skillful means of Vajrayana arise from it. Once we have understood this, it becomes easy to accumulate merit and primordial awareness. Our practice will bring immediate and true results.

We regard all that we experience—sights, sounds, smells, tastes, sensations—as real, existent in fact. This is a kind of fixation. The experience we have of ourselves and things we perceive is the result of these fixations. We believe these things to be really there, really existing. These fixations are the source of much suffering and trouble in our life. Understanding the nature of mind is overcoming these fixations and the consequent suffering they cause. Let us take an example. It is as if the paths in the Sonada area were filled with small briars or thorns, and we were walking barefoot. Small briars and thorns are images of our life. Having to stop and remove each thorn embedded in our feet would make our progress slow and difficult. A first approach to this situation would be to try eliminating the problems one by one, and remove the small briars and thorns from the entire area of Sonada. This would require much effort and time and we would not get very far. It would obviously be easier to wear a pair of strong shoes rather than clear the whole area. With good shoes we can go on all the paths without trouble or hesitation. In the same way, if we really understand the nature of mind, then we understand that all phenomena are empty—simply an illusory interpretation of reality—and that mind itself is empty. If we can realize this illusion and emptiness, we will experience no difficulty in our life, no matter what we do.

THE LAMA IS NOT MATERIAL

Fixations also exist in Dharma practice. When we engage in different practices with faith in relation to the lama, *yidam*, and the Buddha, the Buddha exists, the lama exists, the *yidam* exists. Because they exist, we are able to receive all the forms of blessing and accomplishment they bestow, and realize the true nature of mind. However, what we call the Buddha, or the lama, is not material in the same way as crystal, gold, iron, or stone. You should never think of them with this materialistic attitude. The essence of the lama or Buddha is emptiness; their nature, clarity; their appearance, the play of unimpeded awareness. They have no form, shape, or color, at all—like the empty luminosity of space. When we know them to be like that, we can develop faith, merge our minds with theirs, and let our minds rest peacefully. This attitude and this way of practicing are extremely important.

It is such a vital point! Some people may have great faith in the lama or the Buddha but they think, "My lama is real, he or she really exists. I have great faith in this lama. I love my lama so much. I am very attached to the lama, the focus of my attention. I will do whatever I can to serve the lama, and practice with faith." Then, when the lama dies, they think, "How terrible! My lama has passed away!" They are overcome with sorrow and worry, thinking, "I'll never meet my lama again!" Thus, they become deeply depressed and anxious. This is due to attachment and fixation considering the lama to be materially real.

One of my root lamas was the learned and accomplished lama, Kangyur Rinpoche, an extremely wonderful being. He had a French disciple strongly devoted to him, thinking, "Kangyur Rinpoche is my source lama; I have great trust and faith in him." During meditation instructions, he taught her that she should merge her mind with his. She then thought, "From now on, I shall consider my body and his to be inseparable, our voices and our minds are inseparable." She meditated for some time on this. Her faith was strong, as was her meditation. However, her underlying attachment was intense. After a while, it was as if she were carrying the lama everywhere on her back: wherever she went, he went; where she sat, he sat. She could not separate herself from him and remain alone. She was almost deranged. I used to see her often, but I have not seen her for sometime. I don't know the end of the story.... There is considerable danger in such attachment and fixation on the lama.

As it is said, "If we have attachment to the *yidam*, it is transformed into our greatest fetter. If we have attachment to our accomplishments, they become our greatest obstacles." If we attach ourselves to the *yidam*, it will keep us a prisoner and we will be bound by it. If we are also attached to the accomplishments of practice, they become immense obstacles. Attachment is a mistake.

Many people think, "My lama is getting old, and he lives far away. Because of his old age and the distance, I won't see him again. There is too much distance between us for me to receive his spiritual influence." Another mistake is not knowing that the lama's mind is like the sky and that one's own mind is also like the sky. The impression that the lama is very old or far away, is due to this lack of understanding and wrong view.

In brief, do not think of your body of flesh and blood as truly existent, but consider it as the body of the noble Chenrezig. If you can meditate clearly on the form of Chenrezig, do it. At the very least, simply consider yourself to have that form, an empty appearance. In the same way, you should think of all sound as the union of sound and emptiness, the natural reverberation of the six-syllable mantra of Chenrezig. All mental phenomena and activity should be seen as the mind of Chenrezig, the union of awareness and emptiness—mahamudra. The vastness of space is pervaded by mind and its lucidity.

In whatever we do during the day, recitation of mantra or any other activity, if we know how to keep this awareness of emptiness and space, then attainment of Buddhahood should not present any difficulty.

In this world, every second, someone dies and someone is born. Therefore, this world is constantly changing. In this world, human beings experience many kinds of phenomena, however they all have to undergo birth, old age, illness, and death. Everything is impermanent. Always keep this in mind. It is essential.

March 28, 1989

Index